Irrigation-Induced Water Quality Problems

What Can Be Learned from the San Joaquin Valley Experience

Committee on Irrigation-Induced Water Quality Problems
Water Science and Technology Board
Commission on Physical Sciences, Mathematics, and Resources
National Research Council

NATIONAL ACADEMY PRESS
Washington, D.C. 1989

National Academy Press • 2101 Constitution Avenue, N.W. • Washington, D.C. 20418

NOTICE: The project that is the subject of this report was approved by the Governing Board of the National Research Council, whose members are drawn from the councils of the National Academy of Sciences, the National Academy of Engineering, and the Institute of Medicine. The members of the committee responsible for the report were chosen for their special competences and with regard for appropriate balance.

This report has been reviewed by a group other than the authors according to procedures approved by a Report Review Committee consisting of members of the National Academy of Sciences, the National Academy of Engineering, and the Institute of Medicine.

The National Academy of Sciences is a private, nonprofit, self-perpetuating society of distinguished scholars engaged in scientific and engineering research, dedicated to the furtherance of science and technology and to their use for the general welfare. Upon the authority of the charter granted to it by the Congress in 1863, the Academy has a mandate that requires it to advise the federal government on scientific and technical matters. Dr. Frank Press is president of the National Academy of Sciences.

The National Academy of Engineering was established in 1964, under the charter of the National Academy of Sciences, as a parallel organization of outstanding engineers. It is autonomous in its administration and in the selection of its members, sharing with the National Academy of Sciences the responsibility for advising the federal government. The National Academy of Engineering also sponsors engineering programs aimed at meeting national needs, encourages education and research, and recognizes the superior achievements of engineers. Dr. Robert M. White is president of the National Academy of Engineering.

The Institute of Medicine was established in 1970 by the National Academy of Sciences to secure the services of eminent members of appropriate professions in the examination of policy matters pertaining to the health of the public. The Institute acts under the responsibility given to the National Academy of Sciences by its congressional charter to be an adviser to the federal government and, upon its own initiative, to identify issues of medical care, research, and education. Dr. Samuel O. Thier is president of the Institute of Medicine.

The National Research Council was organized by the National Academy of Sciences in 1916 to associate the broad community of science and technology with the Academy's purposes of furthering knowledge and advising the federal government. Functioning in accordance with general policies determined by the Academy, the Council has become the principal operating agency of both the National Academy of Sciences and the National Academy of Engineering in providing services to the government, the public, and the scientific and engineering communities. The Council is administered jointly by both Academies and the Institute of Medicine. Dr. Frank Press and Dr. Robert M. White are chairman and vice chairman, respectively, of the National Research Council.

Support for this project was provided by the State of California and the U.S. Department of the Interior under Cooperative Agreement No. 5-FC-20-02940.

iii

Preface

Irrigation brings many benefits to society, but it also can bring problems. The irrigation-induced selenium contamination at Kesterson National Wildlife Refuge (NWR) and the ongoing problems with irrigation drainage throughout California's San Joaquin Valley illustrate the conflicts that can arise between the interests of agriculture and the environment. But the events in the San Joaquin Valley also offer insights that can guide decisionmakers in the future as they strive to balance the needs of agriculture and the environment. This report is an attempt to highlight some of those insights.

All decisionmakers face the dilemma of dealing with competing interests—people who see a problem differently and thus seek different solutions. Rarely will decisionmakers find themselves choosing between simple "right" and "wrong" answers; more often they must make complicated judgments and weigh competing values. Maintaining crop production, enhancing wildlife habitats, improving water quality, ensuring public health: these are all admirable goals, but they are not necessarily compatible. More and more, science is playing a critical role in searching for solutions to significant environmental problems and mediating the conflicts that arise.

This committee believes that one step decisionmakers must take to meet this challenge is to evaluate all potential responses openly and fairly. Decisionmakers must make each policy decision in full public view, they must acknowledge the range of options and examine their advantages and disadvantages, and they must honestly identify which parties stand to gain and which stand to lose.

The Committee on Irrigation-Induced Water Quality Problems (Appendix A) was formed in April 1985 to provide ongoing guidance to the San Joaquin Valley Drainage Program (SJVDP), the multiagency team formed to study irrigation in the San Joaquin Valley and search for ways to solve the problems caused by contaminated drainage water. The committee, which operates under the auspices of the National Research Council's Water Science and Technology Board, was also charged to address broader questions and has provided continuing assistance to the U.S. Department of the Interior's National Irrigation Water Quality Program. It has tried to provide a national and future-oriented perspective, one that sees the situation encountered in the San Joaquin Valley as a forewarning of what might be expected to occur elsewhere.

During its original 3-year cooperative agreement period (April 1985 to March 1988), 18 members served on the committee, representing the fields of agricultural engineering, soil science, geochemistry, hydrogeology, ecology, economics, public administration, and other relevant disciplines. When the agreement was extended for 2 additional years in April 1988, one-third of the members rotated off and were replaced, bringing an influx of fresh energy but retaining the needed blend of expertise and experience.

The committee has worked closely with personnel from the SJVDP. The SJVDP is not responsible for the actual cleanup of the Kesterson NWR site but is charged to provide a plan to better manage agricultural drainage in the valley so that similar problems do not continue to occur. The committee provided oversight, evaluated study plans, recommended staff additions, reviewed documents, and made suggestions to improve the caliber of the science and analysis conducted. The committee met frequently with program researchers and managers (Appendix B). The primary product from these activities was advice transmitted through formal National Research Council letter reports (Appendix C).

The San Joaquin Valley Drainage Program is a research team drawn from a number of state and federal agencies with different missions, operating styles, and constituencies. The SJVDP involves the U.S. Bureau of Reclamation, the U.S. Fish and Wildlife Service, and the U.S. Geological Survey, plus the California Department of Fish and Game and the California Department of Water Resources. This diverse group faces a real challenge—to develop an effective, equitable, and scientifically sound solution to a complex, politically charged problem in a relatively short time. Despite their separate and sometimes conflicting missions, they have been asked to work together to develop a proposal that would be accepted by all of the many interests affected.

The Committee on Irrigation-Induced Water Quality Problems elected to write this report to consider how the insights gained through the San Joaquin Valley experience might be applied elsewhere. This document examines the scientific and institutional dimensions of irrigation-induced water quality problems, and it suggests some fundamental elements of good problem solving and policy development that should be considered when similar problems are evaluated in the future. The committee hopes that this effort will be valuable to the people who—at whatever level—must make decisions about irrigation-induced water quality problems in the future, including policymakers; federal, state, and local agency representatives; resource managers; academics; and the public.

Jan van Schilfgaarde, Chairman
Committee on Irrigation-Induced
Water Quality Problems

Contents

Irrigation-Induced Water Quality Problems

Executive Summary

In 1982, scientists made an unexpected discovery at Kesterson National Wildlife Refuge (NWR) in California's San Joaquin Valley. They determined that irrigation drainage water was increasing selenium concentrations in the refuge's ponds and causing reproductive failures and deaths in some species of aquatic organisms and waterfowl.

The rapidity of the contamination was without precedent. From the time the ponds were built in 1971 until 1978, Kesterson's inflow was entirely fresh water. It was exclusively irrigation drainage water by 1981. Barely 2 years later, in 1982, the first problems were noted.

The contaminant involved—selenium—also was unprecedented. In the past, water quality degradation resulting from irrigated agriculture usually was associated with salinity, although residues from fertilizers and pesticides also sometimes caused problems. No one had anticipated contamination by the trace element selenium. Thus the discovery of Kesterson's very visible selenium contamination attracted national attention, and it set in motion a widespread effort to identify causes and remedies.

The refuge's contamination was caused by a combination of natural and human factors—including soils rich in soluble selenium and other trace elements, increased irrigation development with subsequent installation of subsurface drains, and the failure to install an adequate disposal system for the drainage water. Nevertheless, the contamination at Kesterson NWR should not be dismissed as an aberration. Selenium is just one example of a trace element being concentrated as a consequence of irrigation practices.

1

The toxic effects caused by selenium are only symptoms of the range of effects that can be caused by elevated salt concentrations.

The underlying issue is clear: irrigation, like many other uses of water, degrades water quality for later users. The contaminants of concern and the severity of impacts may vary, but the phenomenon of irrigation-induced water quality contamination can no longer be ignored. The degradation at Kesterson NWR and throughout the San Joaquin Valley not only serves as a warning of potential, similar contamination that might occur elsewhere, but it also offers insights about how to study and solve such problems.

In undertaking this report, the National Research Council's Committee on Irrigation-Induced Water Quality Problems sought to provide a discussion of the insights gained from the San Joaquin Valley experience and to highlight some lessons that should not be overlooked when similar environmental problems arise in the future. The committee attempted to focus on questions of a long-term, interdisciplinary nature—ones that address the national public interest—and it wishes to remind scientists, resource managers, politicians, and citizens of the importance of this broad perspective.

This committee was established in April 1985 with the principal purpose of providing the U.S. Department of the Interior and the State of California with assistance in structuring and evaluating a comprehensive research program on irrigation-induced water quality problems in general and the San Joaquin Valley in particular. The committee was charged to (1) review and advise the overall research strategy being conducted by the U.S. Department of the Interior and the State of California; (2) review the research program in progress; and (3) assist in identifying conceptual alternatives available to deal with irrigation drainage problems. The committee met frequently with program managers and researchers from both the San Joaquin Valley Drainage Program and the National Irrigation Water Quality Program (Appendix B) and transmitted advice through formal National Research Council letter reports (Appendix C). The committee elected to publish this report to leave a permanent record of its thinking.

KESTERSON AS AN EXAMPLE OF
A BROADER PROBLEM

The National Research Council's Committee on Irrigation-Induced Water Quality Problems was created as a result of the damage caused by selenium at Kesterson NWR, but it was charged to look beyond the San Joaquin Valley. Kesterson NWR may have become a symbol of this type of water quality problem, but it is not an isolated incident. The U.S. Department of the Interior—through its National Irrigation Water Quality Program—has conducted reconnaissance-level evaluations at more than 20 other sites in the western United States where drainage water from federal irrigation projects flows into wildlife refuges. As of spring 1989, this evaluation process had identified four additional sites that show potential contamination problems and warrant more extensive research. These sites are Stillwater Wildlife Management Area, Nevada; the Salton Sea area, California; Kendrick Reclamation Project area, Wyoming; and the Middle Green River basin area, Utah. Additional sites with similar problems, whether associated with federal water projects or private irrigation development, may be discovered in the future. The potential for such contamination problems elsewhere in the world is also great.

What happened at Kesterson NWR provides one more illustration of the long-known fact that irrigation projects without adequate outlets for drainage create unacceptable levels of salinity. The unexpected part of the scenario was that, given the right soils and geology, the process of drainage on irrigated lands can also concentrate trace elements to levels that can cause real harm to the biota.

UNDERSTANDING THE SCIENTIFIC DIMENSIONS OF AN ENVIRONMENTAL PROBLEM

Decisionmakers must have a basic understanding of the general processes by which irrigation degrades water quality before they can resolve irrigation-induced problems. Hydrological, chemical, geological, and ecological factors all affect and are affected by irrigation. These factors set the stage for the development of problems and are critical to any attempt to select potential solutions, because no solution can be successful unless it reflects some knowledge of the underlying natural processes.

Irrigation causes water quality degradation and salinity problems because all water contains dissolved salts. The concentration of these salts varies depending on the origin of the water. When irrigation water is applied to a field, it moves away by various routes. Some water evaporates from the soil surface; much more is taken up by plants and returned to the atmosphere by plant leaves through transpiration. As both evaporation and transpiration occur, the mineral salts remain behind in the soil. If the salts are not flushed from the root zone by the application of additional irrigation water, the increased salinity will slow plant growth, and in time, agricultural productivity will suffer or cease.

Thus irrigated agriculture will always be short lived unless the salts accumulating in the root zone are flushed or precipitated out. Drainage—whether natural or provided by installing drainage systems—is a necessity to maintain irrigated agriculture over time. In most unaltered ecosystems the common path for soluble salt removal is through the natural drainage provided by rivers and creeks to the ocean. Although the ocean is the ultimate sink for all dissolved salts in the surface drainage system, not all areas drain to the sea in a human time frame. Drainage water sometimes collects in closed basins, as happens in the Dead Sea on the Jordan-Israel border, the Salton Sea in southern California, the Great Salt Lake in Utah, and in the reservoirs at both Stillwater NWR, Nevada, and Kesterson NWR, California.

These natural or human-made low points accumulate both water and salts. The water leads to the growth of wetland vegetation, and this attracts waterfowl and other wildlife. When such enclosed water bodies are used to dispose of irrigation drainage water, they may, through evaporation and other processes, quickly become saline and can ultimately lose their capacity to support biological productivity and diversity. The accumulation of trace elements, some of which are toxic in low concentrations, and of agricultural pollutants, such as pesticides or nitrates and phosphates from fertilizers, can accelerate the deterioration of water quality.

The adverse effects of salinity from irrigation have long been known. The dominant dissolved salt species involved in these processes include the carbonates, bicarbonates, sulfates, and chlorides of sodium, calcium, and magnesium. What has only recently been understood, however, is that potentially serious impacts can be caused by trace elements such as selenium, molybdenum, and arsenic. In most cases, these elements are not carried in by irrigation water but instead originate from in situ geological materials. This has added a new dimension to the problem of irrigation water management. Drainage must now be managed not only to reduce salt accumulation in the root zone and salt disposal in streams, but also to limit the toxic effects of selected trace elements. Given the nation's increased awareness of the values of wetlands, and the increased commitment to environmental values in general, decisionmakers must be prepared to address these irrigation-related problems effectively and equitably.

UNDERSTANDING THE INSTITUTIONAL DIMENSIONS OF AN ENVIRONMENTAL PROBLEM

An array of economic, social, legal, political, and other institutional factors also affects society's perception of irrigation-related problems and their solutions. These factors, however, cannot be considered in isolation because institutional and scientific considerations often are entwined, and effective programs to solve such problems require an understanding of the complex interactions that occur between social and physical components.

The term "institutions" is used broadly in this report to encompass much more than the few government bodies that are directly involved in irrigation-related activities. The concept includes administrative organizations, social customs, regulations, policies, laws, and many other elements. Institutional factors contribute to the creation and continuation of irrigation-induced water quality problems, and they sometimes impede appropriate responses.

The most pervasive economic issue contributing to irrigation-related water quality problems and affecting the choice and success of solutions is the cost of water. The use of subsidies to support the high cost of water projects has brought many benefits to the West, but it has also brought problems. The subsidized low cost of water results in more water being used, encourages farmers to cultivate less desirable lands, and leads to increased agricultural runoff. The difficult question of who will pay for whatever responses are adopted to combat irrigation-related problems must also be addressed. Demographic trends are also important: the West is becoming increasingly urbanized, and this is bringing a shift in priorities for water use. Current water use patterns also diminish the amount of fresh water left in streams to dilute contaminants and carry them to the sea.

The political setting has played a critical role in creating situations conducive to irrigation-related problems. The decision to irrigate the West was, of course, primarily a political one. Policymakers chose to promote social goals—the settlement of the West—through the Reclamation Act of 1902. This occurred at a time when there was great belief in the ability of technology and engineering to overcome almost any natural obstacle. The importance of political, economic, and social factors cannot be overstated. In short, the institutional setting in the West created many of the problems now being faced, it created a structure that prevented the problem from being addressed effectively early on, and it will ultimately determine what solutions will be implemented.

The environmental and social impacts—both positive and negative—associated with irrigation and irrigation drainage water can be exacerbated or ameliorated by the institutional setting. This setting involves a maze of sometimes competing interest groups, agencies, laws, mandates, and social patterns. In many ways, the solutions to irrigation-induced water quality problems are hindered less by scientific and technical uncertainties than they are by conflicts in the social, economic, and legal realms. Thus it will prove impossible to solve these types of problems unless a combination of scientific and institutional means is brought to bear on the process.

RESOLVING PROBLEMS: ESSENTIAL STUDY ELEMENTS

Science now plays a critical role in mediating the conflicts that arise among parties with different perceptions of a problem and its potential resolution. Finding solutions to irrigation-related problems can require difficult choices. Thus the equity and effectiveness of the process used to seek, evaluate, and implement potential solutions become critically important. Sound study design is essential.

A well-conducted problem-solving endeavor should employ, in order, the elements of problem recognition; problem definition; data assessment, collection, and interpretation; identification of alternative responses; and evaluation of those alternatives. In structuring any problem-solving endeavor, explicit attention should be paid to quality assurance and quality control, data and information management, monitoring, risk and exposure assessments, public participation, and conflict management. The complexity of irrigation-related problems should be recognized but should not be used as an excuse for paralysis. And in light of the inherent complexity of such problems, it should be recognized from the start that no environmental problem is solely technical or solely institutional.

A broadly acceptable definition of a recognized problem must be negotiated early in any research effort because different participants will have different perspectives, focus on different symptoms, and have different goals. How a problem is defined ultimately determines the nature of the solutions that are examined and implemented. Obtainable goals can be set only if the problem to be solved is clear and agreed upon by all parties. All potential responses have costs—money, resources, energy, and social costs—so that who will pay becomes an essential consideration. Rarely, if ever, is it possible for all parties to be fully satisfied, and some judgments and compromises will have to be made. If the problem-definition process is adequate, in the end local, regional, and national interests should be appropriately balanced.

Public participation should be incorporated throughout all problem-solving endeavors, but it is particularly necessary when defining a problem and assessing the alternative responses. Public participation brings competing interests together, communicates information, identifies research needs, and helps people understand the nature of scientific uncertainty. In fact, the success of any proposed solution will ultimately depend in large part on the public's confidence that the decision process was open and complete. A wide range of alternative responses needs to be analyzed formally. This not only avoids the pitfall of overlooking important possible solutions, but it also provides a basis for establishing the costs of preferred alternatives compared to the costs of others.

RESOLVING PROBLEMS: IDENTIFYING AND EVALUATING ALTERNATIVES

The goal of all the steps in any problem-solving endeavor is to select and implement successful responses to the defined problem. The process discussed in this report is broadly applicable, whether the problem is caused by irrigation drainage or other influences. Regardless of the specific circumstances, however, one step in this process merits special emphasis: identifying and evaluating the full range of alternative responses available.

To identify appropriate responses—ones that adequately and fairly respond to the stated goals of the problem-solving endeavor—requires careful analysis. Technical, ecological, economic, legal, social, and political criteria all should be evaluated in an attempt to weigh the relative advantages and disadvantages of each proposed approach.

This committee has consistently emphasized the need for decision-makers to display and debate openly the full range of available alternatives before filtering this broad group to a subset of most appropriate options. No potential option should be dismissed a priori, even if intuition judges it to be impractical or unpopular. All options need to be assessed so that the costs and benefits can be compared and so that innovative ideas are not eliminated prematurely. To ignore certain options is to jeopardize the credibility of the overall analysis. Obviously, in the latter stages of any study the time, money, and energy spent assessing the various options will begin to be weighted in favor of the more appropriate choices (after all, this is the objective of the study and evaluation process), but this should never preclude the importance of studying all options before beginning to eliminate unacceptable ones.

The identification and evaluation process should ask and seek answers to difficult questions. These might include the costs and benefits of the option, whether it involves a proven technology, how difficult the option might prove to implement, the time frame of the option, and, importantly, who pays and who benefits. What will emerge from a constructive questioning process will not be one "right" solution but instead a combination of institutional initiatives and technical measures. In the process of formulating this mix, trade-offs associated with different options will become more clear. Legal or political constraints will emerge.

The evaluation of alternatives will involve careful assessment to determine each alternative's role, effectiveness, and incidental impacts in solving a particular environmental problem. Some of the elements to be considered include technical soundness, economic viability, institutional soundness, social acceptability, political feasibility, and ecological appropriateness.

The array of technical and institutional alternatives is formidable. Technical options for salt management, for example, fall generally into three categories (transport and disposal of the drainage water, source control, and treatment of the drainage water) and may include retirement of land from irrigated agriculture, better irrigation management, onsite evaporation ponds, desalinization technologies, chemical and biological removal techniques, ocean disposal, and deep-well injection. Institutional options are particularly diverse. Changes in pricing policy, subsidies, taxation, or water transfer policy will each have impacts. Regulatory approaches can be used, or institutions can be changed to reduce the conflicts caused by conflicting responsibilities.

RECOMMENDATIONS

This committee sees the sometimes negative environmental impacts associated with irrigation in arid regions as a generic problem that the nation must be better prepared to address. In undertaking this report, the National Research Council's Committee on Irrigation-Induced Water Quality Problems sought to help foster awareness of the problems that can be caused by irrigation drainage and to guide decisionmakers in seeking equitable, effective responses. It is virtually inevitable that additional irrigation-related water quality problems will appear in the future, as will other environmental problems of a similar nature, and it would indeed be unfortunate if the insights gained from the San Joaquin Valley experience were to go unrecognized and unheeded.

The recommendations presented here focus on two different levels of activity. The first set of recommendations focuses on planning issues and study design; these recommendations suggest methods that should be used by scientists, resource managers, public officials, citizens, and other decisionmakers when formulating effective responses to irrigation-induced water quality problems wherever they arise. The second set of recommendations addresses policy issues and the opportunities for national action to minimize the negative impacts associated with irrigation.

Planning Issues
Related to Irrigation-Induced Water Quality Problems

• Federal and state agencies should strive to use sound study design when trying to resolve irrigation-induced water quality problems. Sound study design should emphasize a formal systems approach, be responsive to change, and recognize the dynamic properties of the hydrologic system.

• Federal and state agencies responding to irrigation-related problems should develop an action plan that carefully evaluates the alternative responses available and that reflects increasing scientific understanding of ecosystems. They must work to promote public participation, reconcile competing societal needs, balance economic and non-economic costs, and consider the possibility of institutional and legal changes.

• Federal and state agencies should choose a course of action only after all the identified alternatives have been examined and displayed openly. There must be a clear understanding that "win-win" solutions capable of satisfying all parties are rare and that options often need to be site- or region-specific. All options present economic trade-offs and value choices, so that judgments are necessary.

• Federal and state agencies should pay particular attention to the feasibility of implementation. Adequate and stable funding, coordination among agencies and levels of government, effective enforcement, competent personnel with clear responsibilities, and well-defined channels for citizen input are necessary.

• Federal and state agencies need to be actively involved in some type of interagency program to regularly monitor the impacts of irrigation on water quality at all major irrigation projects. This program should contain elements devoted to anticipating future problems and to monitoring water quality over the long term. The National Irrigation Water Quality Program, or some equivalent, could perform these functions indefinitely. Components of the San Joaquin Valley Drainage Program also will need to be continued.

Policy Issues
Related to Irrigation-Induced Water Quality Problems

• If any major irrigation projects are planned in the future, at the onset federal and state agencies should calculate the costs of drainage for irrigation return flows and should commit funds to build and maintain the system.

• Federal and state agencies should design and implement management strategies that minimize the adverse impacts of irrigation, and they must acknowledge the inevitable ecological trade-offs involved.

• Federal and state agencies should systematically monitor all major irrigation projects for substances that could cause water quality problems.

• Federal and state agencies that facilitate or regulate irrigation should periodically calculate and publicize the associated environmental costs as well as the agricultural benefits, and should work to accommodate the nation's increasing commitment to protecting environmental values.

• Irrigation return flows should not be exempt from federal and state water quality regulations, and such regulations should be enforced.

• Federal and state agencies should increase their efforts to provide water supplies for wildlife, enhance wildlife habitats, and protect the biological and recreational values associated with in-stream flows and good water quality.

• Federal and state agencies should acknowledge all external costs— including social and environmental costs—when calculating the costs and benefits of agricultural subsidies.

• Federal and state agencies should identify irrigated lands that are degrading water quality significantly and should implement cost-effective, environmentally sound actions to correct or minimize the degradation. Such a program would incorporate a range of alternative approaches for preventing, mitigating, and treating irrigation drainage problems. This would include, if necessary, phasing out production on particularly problematic lands.

Responding to Irrigation-Induced Water Quality Problems: A Shared Responsibility

One fact made clear during this committee's oversight of the San Joaquin Valley Drainage Program is that finding a solution to the valley's drainage problem, and any such situation anywhere in the West or the world, is not a purely technical question. Indeed, the more difficult issues are often political, social, and economic. In all cases, however, the various components are intimately interrelated. Only by defining and addressing the system as a whole, and realistically assessing its complexity, can progress toward real and lasting solutions be made.

The U.S. Bureau of Reclamation, which has received considerable attention in this report because of its primary role in the Kesterson NWR experience, is not alone in facing the significant challenges arising from irrigation-induced water quality problems. The problems are not all caused by federal and state activities, nor can they necessarily be solved at those levels alone. The federal and state agencies involved in irrigation are mandated to carry out the will of the public, and so the ultimate responsibility for solving these types of problems is one that the public shares.

1
Introduction: Kesterson as an Example of a Broader Problem

In 1982, scientists discovered that irrigation drainage water had contaminated the ponds at Kesterson National Wildlife Refuge (NWR) in California with toxic levels of selenium, a naturally occurring trace element (Presser and Ohlendorf, 1987). Waterfowl were dying and suffering reproductive failures; reduced fish populations, algal blooms, and dwindling cattails all indicated a problem of serious proportions.

The discovery of Kesterson's selenium contamination set in motion a chain of events that is still progressing today. Farmers, scientists, engineers, policymakers, and various special interest groups—both from California and from around the nation—have become involved in a long process of trying to understand and solve the problem. Countless meetings have been held, and dozens of studies have been produced. The incident garnered national attention and sparked public recognition that irrigation-induced water quality problems are affecting much of the West as well as other regions where irrigation is practiced.

Scientists and policymakers involved in this search for answers face three distinctly different scales of activity. They must decide how to clean up the contamination at Kesterson NWR, how to prevent similar problems throughout the San Joaquin Valley where Kesterson is located (Figure 1.1), and how to address this generic type of problem in the West and elsewhere. This last question is perhaps the most troubling; although the contaminants of concern and the severity of impacts may vary, irrigation drainage is causing contamination problems at other national wildlife refuges and in

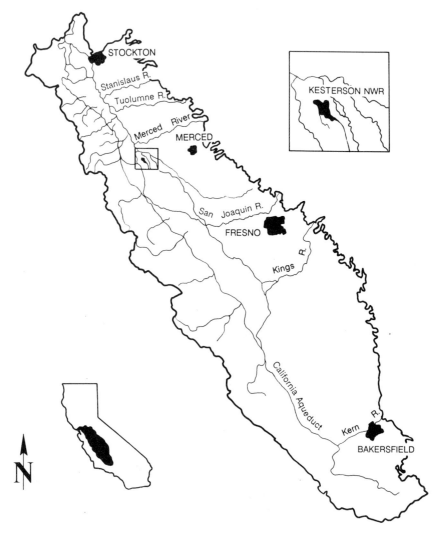

FIGURE 1.1   The San Joaquin Valley, site of Kesterson National Wildlife Refuge and focus of the San Joaquin Valley Drainage Program.
SOURCE: Courtesy of the San Joaquin Valley Drainage Program.

other natural habitats (Deason, 1989).   The phenomenon of irrigation-induced water quality contamination can be ignored no longer.

Kesterson NWR has become a symbol of this type of water quality problem, but it is not an aberration. The U.S. Department of the Interior's National Irrigation Water Quality Program has surveyed a number of other refuges that receive irrigation drainage water and has identified at least

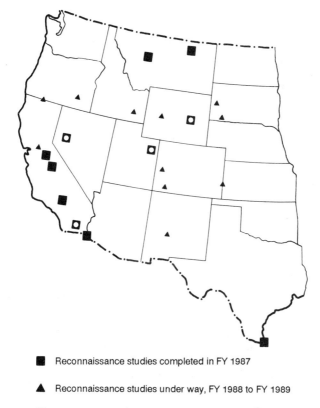

■   Reconnaissance studies completed in FY 1987

▲   Reconnaissance studies under way, FY 1988 to FY 1989

□   Detailed studies under way FY 1988 to FY 1989 *

* These sites were also reconnaissance study sites.

FIGURE 1.2 Sites being studied for potential irrigation drainage problems by the U.S. Department of the Interior, 1986 to 1990.
SOURCE: Courtesy of the U.S. Department of the Interior.

four other sites that may have reached unacceptable levels of contamination (Figure 1.2). The Stillwater Wildlife Management area in Nevada (personal communication from R. Hoffman, U.S. Geological Survey, Carson City, Nev., 1989), the Salton Sea area in California (personal communication from J. Setmire, U.S. Geological Survey, San Diego, Calif., 1989), the Middle Green River basin area in Utah (Stephens et al., 1988), and the Kendrick Reclamation Project area in Wyoming (Peterson et al., 1988) have shown preliminary signs of contamination and are all undergoing in-depth study. More problem sites may be identified as other reconnaissance studies continue. Although the U.S. Department of the Interior does not believe the evidence points to an environmental problem of catastrophic proportions, it does agree that some problems of significant magnitude do exist and should be addressed (Deason, 1989). Also, the potential for problems on privately irrigated lands remains unexplored.

The degradation at Kesterson NWR and throughout the San Joaquin Valley not only serves as a warning of the potential for irrigation-induced contamination, but it also offers insights about how to study and respond to such problems. This report is an attempt to highlight some of these lessons. This chapter introduces the setting and the participants involved in the search for solutions to the irrigation-induced water quality problems found in California's San Joaquin Valley. It begins by reviewing the role of water development in the West and then focuses on the San Joaquin Valley and the selenium contamination discovered there. Later chapters highlight the nature of good problem solving and the technical and institutional lessons to be drawn from the San Joaquin Valley experience.

WESTERN U.S. AGRICULTURE

Understanding the history of irrigation in the West can help explain today's irrigation-related problems, both the causes and why the solutions are so difficult. Agriculture in the western United States has long been inextricably tied to irrigation. Many cultures throughout history—Native American, Mexican, and European—have inhabited the arid West, each practicing some form of irrigated agriculture. Whether by capturing flash floods with simple check dams in desert arroyos or by building elaborate networks of impoundments and canals to serve thousands of acres of cropland, irrigation perturbs natural systems. It also leaves its imprint on social systems. Irrigation has had a profound impact in shaping western economies, social structures, laws, and politics. These antecedent events limit what can be done now to solve irrigation-induced problems.

Western water law was shaped by the needs of mining and agriculture. Early precedents applied similarly to both ore and water: to obtain rights to a resource, the first claimant prevailed (appropriative rights). First, an informal body of water law evolved to serve the mining camps. As the West grew and codified its water rights system, the specifics were refined, and some states incorporated aspects of riparian water law from the East, but the basic philosophy remained. "Beneficial use" became the basis for an appropriator's water right. Custom and tradition dictated the quantity considered reasonable. A person could lose a water right if the water was not put to a beneficial use—hence the admonition, "use it or lose it" (El-Ashry and Gibbons, 1986).

In the nineteenth century, the federal government allocated public lands freely or very cheaply to private ownership to stimulate western settlement. Much irrigable land in the West passed into private ownership under public land laws such as the Desert Land Act of 1877, reflecting the federal objective to have the West occupied and developed. When private capital and local public resources were unable to sustain the large-scale water development desired in some areas, the nation initiated a reclamation program in 1902 with the goal of "making the deserts bloom." Policymakers hoped that inexpensive water would foster new communities of family farms in the 17 western states. The Reclamation Act of 1902 marked the beginning of many decades of federal involvement in building and subsidizing irrigation projects in the West.

Today, irrigation consumes the majority of the West's water. Including both public and private developments, irrigation accounts for about 90 percent of the water consumed in the West (U.S. Geological Survey, 1983). In California, 83 percent of all consumptive water use is accounted for by agriculture (California Department of Water Resources, 1987). The scale of irrigation has grown impressively in the United States: in 1890, the nation had about 4 million irrigated acres; by 1977, it had 60 million acres, with about 50 million acres located in the 17 western states. Irrigated farms contribute more than one-fourth of the nation's total value of crop production, even though they constitute only one-seventh of all agricultural lands (Frederick and Hanson, 1984). The U.S. Bureau of Reclamation (USBR) provided water to more than 12 million acres in 1986, supplying about 25 percent of the West's irrigation water (U.S. Bureau of Reclamation, 1984). (The USBR is responsible for only about one-fourth of the nation's irrigation projects, but it is involved in the largest developments.)

Irrigation is essential to the West's agricultural economy, but water use for agriculture is not expected to grow significantly. Total irrigated area in the West has declined since 1979 (with the exception of 1982), whereas land used for other purposes (e.g., residential, commercial, and industrial) has increased (U.S. Bureau of Reclamation, 1984). Urbanization and industrial development bring pressures to retire irrigated acreage, and this trend is likely to continue.

The greatest irrigation-related threat to western agriculture is increasing salinity. Increased salinity is an unavoidable by-product of irrigation because all water carries dissolved salts, and as the water evaporates, the salts are left behind (see Chapter 2). An estimated one-fourth, and possibly up to one-third, of the irrigated lands in the United States suffer some damage from salinity. This damage includes reductions in yield, restrictions on choice of crops that can be grown, or need for increased management expertise (van Schilfgaarde and Rhoades, 1984). Salinity affects nonagricultural users as well, such as households, water utilities, and industry.

The Colorado River basin (including the Imperial and Coachella Valleys of southern California that receive Colorado River water) faces the

The opening of the West was sparked in large part by the development of irrigation. When the Reclamation Act of 1902 was passed, the goal was to "make the deserts bloom" and encourage farmers to settle the vast, dry landscape. Today, the U.S. Bureau of Reclamation provides water to more than 12 million acres, including 105,000 acres of land served by the Owyhee Dam in Oregon.
CREDIT: U.S. Bureau of Reclamation, J. D. Roderick.

West's greatest salinity problems, followed by the Rio Grande basin of New Mexico and Texas and the Central Valley of California, including the San Joaquin Valley (U.S. Environmental Protection Agency, 1974). The Colorado River basin provides an example of the scale of the problem: agriculture there is estimated to have lost between $113 million and $122 million per year between 1976 and 1985 because of salinity (Lohman et al., 1988).

THE SAN JOAQUIN VALLEY

The San Joaquin Valley lies in the southern half of California's great Central Valley and extends approximately 250 miles from the Tahachapi Mountains to the San Joaquin-Sacramento River Delta. The valley averages about 50 miles in width, flanked on the east by the Sierra Nevada mountains and on the west by the low-lying Coast Range (Letey et al., 1986). It is a region of fertile soils, but historically it suffered from seasonal water shortages and periodic flooding. The valley's extensive wetlands made it an early candidate for the development of irrigated agriculture. At first, farmers borrowed techniques used by miners to move water to their claims. As time went on, methods became more sophisticated and coordinated. Farmers irrigated by managing the water yielded by the Sierra Nevada mountains to the east and, later, by importing water from farther north. As is discussed later in this chapter, individuals grouped together in reclamation and irrigation districts, and plans for a major water delivery system were proposed as early as 1873 (California State Department of Public Works, 1932).

Even before the turn of the century, however, agricultural experts recognized that irrigated agriculture could be of only short duration if provisions were not made to dispose of the brackish drainage water. As E. W. Hilgard, an early soil scientist, geographer, and professor said of California in 1886:

> It is hardly necessary to go further into the details (of the problems occurring in India) to enforce the lesson and warning they convey to our irrigating communities. . . . The evils now besetting (California's irrigation districts) are already becoming painfully apparent; and to expect them not to increase unless the proper remedies are applied is to hope that natural laws will be waived in favor of California. The natural conditions under which the irrigation canals of India have brought about the scourge, are exactly reproduced in the great valley of California; and what has happened in India will assuredly happen there also. (Hilgard, 1886)

Today, the San Joaquin Valley contains 4.7 million acres of irrigated farmland, the largest concentration of irrigated land in California (California Department of Water Resources, 1987). It is still a fertile region that supplies the nation with a great variety of agricultural products. And Professor Hilgard's comments about salinity, its effects on crops, and the importance of appropriate management practices provide a foreshadowing of the irrigation and drainage problems now being faced (Letey et al., 1986).

The Natural History of the San Joaquin Valley

The San Joaquin Valley has a Mediterranean climate. Summers are hot and dry; fall is a time of stable temperatures and low moisture levels. Winter temperatures are mild but not warm enough to grow crops. Winter can bring periods of dense fog and intense storms from the Pacific, but most of the precipitation falls as rain on the western slopes of the Coast Range before it can reach the valley floor. Winter rainfall rarely exceeds 10 in. on the west side of the valley, and the drier eastern slopes of the Coast Range generate little runoff and experience almost no snow.

The snowpack in the Sierra Nevada mountains stores the equivalent of as much as 40 in. of water during the winter months and is more

The San Joaquin Valley in California contains 4.7 million acres of irrigated farmland and supplies the nation with a great variety of agricultural products. The U.S. Bureau of Reclamation's Central Valley Project includes 102 miles of canal and irrigates an area 65 miles long and averaging 13 miles wide.
CREDIT: U.S. Bureau of Reclamation, J. C. Dahilig.

important than direct precipitation to the basin's hydrologic budget. When temperatures rise in the spring, snowmelt runoff from the Sierra Nevada increases the flow of streams into the valley, generally providing dependable supplies of water well into the summer. Peak stream discharges occur in April, May, and June. The low-water period begins in August and extends through February. Heavy rains can cause major flood peaks beginning as early as November.

The native ecological communities of the San Joaquin Valley reflect this blend of climate, terrain, soil, and hydrology. Broad belts of vegetation generally extend from north to south, reflecting gradients of precipitation. Species diversity and biomass increase away from the valley floor in response to precipitation and elevation.

The dominant ground cover in central California before the Europeans arrived in the late eighteenth century consisted of perennial grasses, herbs, forbs, and shrubs. Deciduous trees grew in scattered locations where local conditions were favorable. Large wetland areas along the central floor of the San Joaquin Valley were seasonally or permanently flooded. The natural community types that predominated in the valley included savanna, riparian forest, prairie desert saltbush, spiny saltbush, marsh, lowland heath, and oak woodlands. These communities were home to a variety of native mammals, including pronghorn antelope, tule elk, mule deer, grey wolves, coyotes, and abundant small mammals, birds, and insects (Ogden, 1988).

Agricultural development required the removal of native flora and displaced the fauna. In addition, actions to control pests harmed many species directly and others indirectly by affecting their food sources. Although many wildlife species still reside in the valley, in general their populations have diminished. Wetland habitats in California's Central Valley have been reduced greatly from historical levels of about 4 million acres to the present level of about 300,000 to 400,000 acres (SJVDP, 1987a). Thus the remaining wetlands, including evaporation ponds and other water storage facilities created for agriculture, are increasingly attractive to wildlife.

There are 10 national wildlife refuges and 4 state wildlife management areas in California's Central Valley. These areas provide about one-third of the state's waterfowl habitat. For years these areas have been sustained by surplus irrigation water, irrigation return flow, and ground water. As California's demand for fresh water has grown, the quantity and quality of the water delivered to these wildlife habitats have diminished, especially during periods of lower than average rainfall. State and federal agencies have estimated that these areas need a water supply of more than 500,000 acre-feet annually to sustain them adequately; at present, average annual water deliveries total about 380,000 acre-feet (California Department of Water Resources, 1987).

Differences Between the East and West Sides of the San Joaquin Valley

The hydrology and agricultural economies of the east and west sides of the San Joaquin Valley are markedly different. Irrigation generally developed earlier (in the late 1800s) on the east side of the valley, where there was an abundance of water from the Sierra Nevada. Furthermore, ground water was available for irrigation at relatively shallow depths. The salt concentrations from both of these sources were low because parent rock on the east side is granitic. Where excessive irrigation water was applied, waterlogged soils became apparent by the turn of the century. Development of numerous large-capacity wells by the 1920s lowered water levels, however, and forestalled drainage problems.

Farmers on the east side historically have had smaller, family-run farms, and they have lived on their land. Most of the domestic water supply (including municipal and industrial supplies) on the east side historically has been supplied by ground water. Conjunctive use, a system combining surface water from a canal, the pumping of ground water, and induced ground water recharge, has been practiced recently on the east side to maintain relatively stable ground water levels.

Farms on the west side historically have been larger and have been operated by managers who often do not live on the farms. The initial development of irrigation on the west side of the San Joaquin Valley depended primarily on ground water. Farmers commonly tap the deeper ground water (between about 400 and 2500 ft in depth) recharged from the mountains because shallow ground water often has high salinity. Also, large-scale overdrafting of the ground water has lowered the water table.

Before water was imported from northern California, well capacity and water quality constrained many farmers on the valley's west side in their choice of crops and how much land they could irrigate. Also, the parent rock on the west side is of marine origin and contributes salts to the soils and ground water (Presser and Ohlendorf, 1987). The cost of correcting these problems generally was prohibitive. When a new source of water became available through the San Luis Unit of the Central Valley Project, ground water pumping essentially ceased because the imported water was of much better quality and was cheaper.

Once ground water pumping stopped and imported water was available, another type of hydrologic imbalance developed. The importation of low-cost water led to a high level of use, and the level of the water tables in the region—which had been overdrawn for decades—rose. Drainage problems, predicted decades earlier, soon emerged, and efforts were started to provide a drainage canal (Dudek and Horner, 1981).

KESTERSON NATIONAL WILDLIFE REFUGE

Kesterson NWR is located on the west side of the San Joaquin Valley. At the time the selenium contamination was discovered there in 1982, the refuge was made up of 12 evaporation ponds—collectively called Kesterson Reservoir—with an average depth of 3 to 4 ft and a total water surface area of about 1200 acres when filled.

The problems at Kesterson NWR evolved in part because of the refuge's convoluted history (Table 1.1). Kesterson NWR was planned originally as a storage area to be used to control water flowing down the proposed San Luis Drain into the western part of the Sacramento/San Joaquin Delta and ultimately to the San Francisco Bay (Ohlendorf, 1989). Its use as a wildlife refuge was opportunistic. However, the drain was never extended past Kesterson NWR for political and social reasons, and the reservoir came to serve two purposes. It was used as a large evaporation pond to dispose of agricultural drainage water, and it provided wildlife habitat.

The ponds at Kesterson NWR were completed in 1971 at a cost of about $10 million. Between 1971 and 1978 all the water flowing into the Kesterson ponds was fresh; by 1981, the inflow was exclusively subsurface agricultural drainage water. The mineral content (including selenium) in the reservoir increased as water entered and evaporated (Letey et al., 1986).

The U.S. Fish and Wildlife Service (USFWS) first noticed problems at Kesterson NWR in 1982: large-mouth and striped bass, catfish, and carp had disappeared (Ohlendorf, 1984). In the spring of 1983, eggs from water birds exhibited decreased hatchability and deformities of the embryos. The cause was determined to be elevated levels of selenium, a common, naturally occurring trace element, which was being carried into the reservoir in agricultural drainage water and concentrated through natural processes (Presser and Barnes, 1984).

The roots of this problem go back to the historical development of irrigation in California. Calls for large-scale irrigation, of course, go far back in the history of California's settlement (California State Department of Public Works, 1932). When several years of drought struck in the early 1920s, California legislators proposed a massive water project consisting of dams, canals, and drains so that agriculture could prosper in spite of the vagaries of the natural water supply. The short-term water shortage was a greater concern than the long-term threat to the region's agriculture from salinity, even though the need for salt management and drainage was recognized. The Central Valley Project was first proposed in the 1930s. Originally, California had planned to build the project—an ambitious plan including dams, canals, drains, and other structures—but during the Depression the state could not raise bond monies and the federal government assumed responsibility for its construction. Management responsibility was assigned to the USBR.

In 1943 the Westside Landowners Association (later to become the Westlands Water District) asked the USBR to investigate the possibility of getting a more reliable water supply for the west side of the valley. A feasibility study was completed in 1956, and in response to these requests, Congress authorized construction of the San Luis Unit of the Central Valley Project in 1960. This project was ultimately to deliver 1.2 million acre-feet of water each year to Westlands Water District. The plans included a drainage system discharging into the Sacramento/San Joaquin Delta and ultimately into San Francisco Bay.

The building of the San Luis Drain was controversial from the beginning. In 1965, the California legislature had responded to growing

TABLE 1.1 A Chronology of Selected San Joaquin Valley Events, 1937 to 1989

Date	Description
1937	Delta-Mendota Project is authorized by Congress.
1950	Delta-Mendota Service Area water deliveries begin.
1957	California releases plans for federal-state San Joaquin Valley Master Drain.
1960	Congress authorizes San Luis Unit, including the San Luis Drain, to carry irrigation waste water out of the Central Valley and discharge it into San Francisco Bay.
1966	Congress requires an agreement between the United States and California regarding a discharge point for the San Luis Drain. Water quality studies are also mandated.
1967	State abandons role in valley master drain.
1968	Water deliveries start in the San Luis Service Area and U.S. Bureau of Reclamation (USBR) begins construction of San Luis Drain and Kesterson Reservoir.
1969	USBR and U.S. Fish and Wildlife Service (USFWS) agree to operate Kesterson Reservoir as a waterfowl management area.
1970	USFWS expresses concern about the degradation of ground water by nitrates in the San Joaquin Valley and its subsequent effect on the San Joaquin River.
1971	Kesterson Reservoir is completed at a cost of $10 million.
1971-1978	Kesterson Reservoir inflow consists of fresh water.
1975	Funding limitations and environmental concerns stop construction of the San Luis Drain north of Kesterson Reservoir.
1975	San Joaquin Valley Interagency Drainage Program (SJVIDP), a precursor to the San Joaquin Valley Drainage Program, is established. Limited testing for trace elements is conducted, but tests for selenium are not included.
1979	SJVIDP issues report recommending that no drain construction north of the reservoir occur until USBR has completed the final supplemental environmental impact statement for the San Luis Unit. Subsurface drainage water begins to flow into Kesterson.
1981	All water coming into Kesterson consists of irrigation drainage water. USBR imposes moratorium on additional farm drainage connections to San Luis Drain because of limited capacity at Kesterson Reservoir.

TABLE 1.1 (continued)

Date	Description
1982	First observations of biological changes in reservoir ponds (e.g., dying cattails, algal blooms, declining use by waterfowl). USFWS biologists find high levels of selenium in mosquito fish. Preliminary toxicity data are provided to USBR. USBR questions the data and USFWS asks the U.S. Geological Survey (USGS) for help.
1983	USFWS biologists conclude that dead and deformed bird embryos resulted from high selenium levels. USBR officials dispute findings. The California Water Resources Control Board is informed. The California Department of Public Health issues notice limiting waterfowl consumption from the Kesterson area, and USFWS closes Kesterson ponds to public access.
1984	A state-federal team, the San Joaquin Valley Drainage Program (SJVDP) is created to develop alternative solutions to San Joaquin Valley salinity problems. A Kesterson area duck club owner files suit against USBR and state agencies for damage to his property. USFWS begins intensive hazing (harassing the birds so they move on to other habitat) to prevent migratory waterfowl from being exposed to selenium at Kesterson. State Water Resources Control Board hearings begin.
1985	U.S. Department of the Interior (DOI) announces plans to close Kesterson Reservoir and San Luis Drain and to terminate irrigation deliveries to 42,000 acres in Westlands Water District. Later, a compromise allows additional time to end irrigation drainage.
1986	Drainage flows to Kesterson are stopped. USBR proposes a phased cleanup approach.
1987	State Water Resources Control Board (SWRCB) orders onsite disposal of Kesterson waste, rejecting an alternative federal proposal. An onsite disposal facility is to be completed by August 1988.
1988	DOI petitions SWRCB for another hearing on Kesterson cleanup, presents evidence that onsite disposal will create new problems, and asks for time to conduct further research. Onsite approach is dropped, and DOI is ordered to fill and grade Kesterson. Hazing continues where necessary.
1989	SJVDP continues to develop alternative solutions to deal with irrigation-induced water quality problems in the San Joaquin Valley. Work to fill and grade the ponds at Kesterson is completed. Biological and ground water monitoring continues. The USBR submits its plan for the future maintenance of the Kesterson area to the SWRCB, projecting a continued need for management, monitoring, and some experimentation.

SOURCE: Developed from Letey et al., 1986.

The current awareness of irrigation-induced water quality problems arose when scientists discovered that irrigation drainage water was leading to reproductive failures and deaths in some species of aquatic organisms and waterfowl at Kesterson National Wildlife Refuge. The ponds at Kesterson were built to serve as temporary storage areas for drainage water but the reservoir came to serve as a large evaporation pond. Since the discovery of toxic effects caused by increased concentrations of the trace element selenium, the water in these ponds has been drained and the low-lying areas filled.
CREDIT: U.S. Fish and Wildlife Service, G. Zahm.

public concern about potential pollution in the San Francisco Bay and had requested a comprehensive study of the estuary. In 1967, citing budget constraints, the state decided not to participate in the drainage project.

Nevertheless, USBR decided to proceed and began building the San Luis Drain in 1968. By 1970, proceeding under the commonly accepted assumption that drainage waters were suitable for waterfowl and other wildlife, the USBR had signed a management agreement with the USFWS to manage the wetland habitat that would be created. The wildlife refuge aspects of the project, however, were incidental to the main function of regulating the drain-water flow. As planned, the San Luis Drain was to conduct drainage water to the ponds at Kesterson NWR and then on to the

San Francisco Bay. The first phase of construction, however, included only the southern half of the drain. Until the drain was completed, the ponds at Kesterson NWR were to serve as a temporary holding area to dispose of the collected agricultural drainage by evaporation and percolation.

The decision to build the drain from the valley toward the outlet, rather than from the outlet toward the lands to be drained, was a political decision that later proved to be a strategic mistake. The decision was based on the assumption that authorization and funding to complete the drain would eventually be available, an assumption that proved wrong in the face of changing economic, political, and environmental attitudes.

Meanwhile, the National Environmental Policy Act of 1970 had become law, and the USBR released the required environmental impact statement for the drain in 1972. Although the statement supported the Sacramento/San Joaquin Delta outlet, law suits were filed, and a task force was established to review the San Luis Unit. Meanwhile, subsurface drains continued to be installed on farms in the region, and by 1981 the drainage water volume reaching the ponds at Kesterson NWR had increased to approximately 7000 acre-feet/yr—the upper limit that could be evaporated or otherwise disposed of at Kesterson.

In 1986, the USBR informed water users in the area served by the drain that it was placing a moratorium on the connection of any additional on-farm drains to the district's collector system until Kesterson NWR was enlarged or the drain was completed to the delta. By 1987, the issue was moot. Plans were made to keep wildlife from using the area while an effective method of cleanup for the contaminated soils was sought. After much deliberation and debate, in 1988 the U.S. Department of the Interior was ordered to fill and grade Kesterson, a task that was completed in early 1989. The total cleanup costs are estimated to be more than $47 million (personal communication from J. P. Deason, U.S. Department of the Interior, Washington, D.C., 1989). For at least 5 more years, biological and ground water monitoring will continue, as will some experimentation and management at the site, bringing continued additional costs that are projected to be about $3.5 million per year.

STATE AND FEDERAL INVOLVEMENT

The contamination at Kesterson NWR has influenced events far beyond the confines of the San Joaquin Valley. Local residents, special interest groups, state and federal agencies, and elected officials have all been involved. These diverse groups often have conflicting interests. Some want action quickly, whereas others seek long-term solutions. Refuge managers want to protect wildlife now and provide safe habitats for the long term; farmers want to continue to farm and want drainage for waterlogged fields. Hunters and wildlife advocates want an assured supply of water to support wildlife populations. Political leaders worry about the issue of who pays and who benefits.

The three federal agencies most active in resolving the San Joaquin Valley drainage issue are in the U.S. Department of the Interior: the U.S. Geological Survey (USGS), the USFWS, and the USBR. The USGS is an earth science information and research organization, and its role is to collect data to understand the geology and hydrology of the valley. The USGS first identified the high concentrations of selenium that had accumulated in the ponds at Kesterson NWR (Presser and Barnes, 1984). Their research on selenium and other trace elements has provided an important underpinning for the search for options to resolve the valley's drainage problems.

The U.S. Fish and Wildlife Service is the federal government's lead agency for conserving and managing the nation's fish and wildlife resources. Its mandate ranges from managing almost 90 million acres of land in the National Wildlife Refuge System, to conserving plant and animal species threatened with extinction, to advising other federal agencies on how to manage wildlife on their lands, to enforcing federal wildlife laws and international wildlife treaties. It has a long-standing focus on game species. The USFWS's mandated responsibility in the Kesterson situation is to protect the fish and wildlife, a responsibility that has at times brought the USFWS into conflict with other interests in the San Joaquin Valley.

The other major federal participant in the San Joaquin Valley is the USBR. The USBR, as mentioned earlier, was established under the Reclamation Act of 1902 to provide irrigation and drainage to reclaim the desert lands of the West. In recent years, with much of its development mission fulfilled, the USBR has increasingly come under criticism for being slow to adapt to the public's increasing environmental awareness and demands for improved management and nonstructural solutions to water problems.

A historical conflict exists between the USFWS and the USBR because of their differing missions. The USBR has had the political influence to prevail in most disputes. This history of conflict has made the multiagency program of the San Joaquin Valley Drainage Program, discussed later in this chapter, particularly difficult to manage. Curiously, neither the U.S. Department of Agriculture nor the U.S. Environmental Protection Agency has been active in the program, despite the obvious relevance of their missions.

The main California state agencies involved with the San Joaquin Valley Drainage Program are the Department of Water Resources (DWR) and the Department of Fish and Game (DFG). The DWR is a natural resource management agency with responsibilities for activities relating to water quantity and distribution. The DFG is the state counterpart of the USFWS, with wildlife management and state-level enforcement responsibilities.

Local agencies also have key roles. The county health departments of Fresno and Merced Counties have jurisdiction over individual domestic wells, well drilling permits for all wells (including monitoring wells), and public nuisances, such as odors. Government agencies in both Fresno County (where Westlands Water District and the primary drainage problem area are located) and Merced County (where Kesterson NWR is located) have been active participants.

Another important state agency is the California State Water Resources Control Board (SWRCB), which is responsible for water quality regulation. The Regional Water Quality Control Board, Central Valley region, is a branch of the SWRCB with its own board and staff in Sacramento and Fresno. The regional board has substantial authority to protect the quality of surface water and ground water in the Central Valley. It issues waste discharge permits, requires monitoring programs at many sites, and is involved with numerous site-specific cleanups of soil and ground water contamination. It implements, at a regional level, numerous state regulatory programs. (These programs and related federal legislation are described in Chapter 3.)

The Department of Water Resources has not played a major role in the Kesterson NWR experience because the reservoir did not receive drainage from any state projects. The DWR is, however, a participant in drainage problems in state water service areas, such as in Kern and Tulare Counties. The DWR has conducted drainage research, including the construction of a pilot plant for treating drainage water, and has monitored the quality of subsurface drainage water in the San Joaquin Valley. It routinely monitors surface water and ground water in many parts of California, and it serves as a repository for information on water distribution and quality in the state.

THE SAN JOAQUIN VALLEY DRAINAGE PROGRAM

The San Joaquin Valley Drainage Program (SJVDP) was established in mid-1984 as a cooperative program to unite the efforts of the primary state and federal agencies involved in solving the valley's irrigation-related problems. (As a regulatory agency, SWRCB does not participate.) The program is scheduled to complete its tasks and go out of existence in October 1990. The purposes of the program are to study the problems associated with irrigation drainage on the west side of the San Joaquin Valley and to recommend immediate and long-term management alternatives to achieve an equitable balance between irrigated agriculture and its associated environmental impacts. The SJVDP has defined four primary objectives that reflect the competing missions of the agencies involved (SJVDP, 1987a):

- Minimize potential health risks that may be associated with agricultural drainage water.
- Protect existing and future reasonable and beneficial uses of surface and ground waters.
- Sustain productivity of existing farmlands on the west side of the San Joaquin Valley.
- Protect and enhance fish and wildlife resources.

The organization of the SJVDP consists of six main elements and several related independent programs (Figure 1.3). Staff for the interagency study team are drawn from the participating agencies. Of the six main elements, the Intergovernmental Coordination Team is composed of policy-level appointees of the secretary of the interior and the governor of California. This group provides broad guidance on program objectives, makes major policy decisions, and reviews overall progress. In this role, it has not participated in the program's day-to-day activities.

The Policy and Management Committee (PMC), in contrast, plays an active role in the SJVDP process and has been closely involved in resolving the valley's drainage-related problems. The PMC provides specific guidance on program direction and priorities, allocates funds and personnel, and acts on recommendations from the Interagency Study Team and advisory groups. In effect, the PMC serves as the SJVDP's board of directors. The PMC is made up of three federal agency regional or district directors and two directors of California state departments. State and federal regulatory agencies (including the U.S. Environmental Protection Agency) declined representation on the PMC to eliminate any potential conflicts of interest.

The Interagency Study Team is a task force responsible for gathering and analyzing technical data and ultimately for formulating and evaluating alternate plans for managing the valley's drainage-related problems. This group is headed by a program manager who is responsible to the chairman of the PMC. Support is provided by a deputy program manager, agency representatives, and various scientific and support staff.

The Citizens' Advisory Committee was established in 1987 by the California DWR to facilitate public participation in the SJVDP's problem-solving endeavor. The committee consists of 14 people representing various affected organizations and geographical regions. The Citizens' Advisory Committee has taken on the task of helping the SJVDP implement its public participation plan, and it provides comments on draft SJVDP documents.

The Interagency Technical Advisory Committee consists of outside scientists who provide technical advice to the SJVDP. Unlike the PMC, this body includes representatives of regulatory agencies as well as the California university system. Seven technical subcommittees provide direct

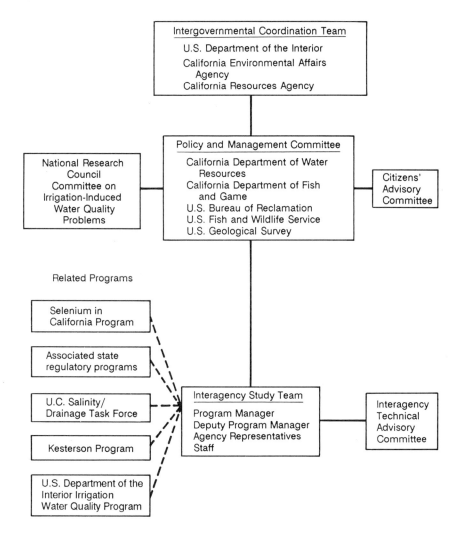

FIGURE 1.3 San Joaquin Valley Drainage Program organization chart.
SOURCE: SJVDP, 1987b.

support on data management, estuary and ocean biology, geochemistry, on-farm management, public health, drainage water treatment and disposal, and valley biology. An ad hoc working group also has been established to deal with quality assurance and quality control issues.

Finally, this committee, the Committee on Irrigation-Induced Water Quality Problems, serves as a source of scientific guidance for the SJVDP. (See Appendix A for biographical sketches of committee members.) The involvement of the National Research Council (NRC) provides a national perspective on the problems in the San Joaquin Valley and gives access to a broad range of scientific expertise.

A number of subcommittees back up the NRC committee, providing specialized assistance when needed to address areas such as data management, economics and policy, systems analysis, public health, quality assurance and quality control, and treatment technologies. These subcommittees were most active in the early stages of the SJVDP, although the Subcommittee on Economics, Policy, and Systems Analysis and the Subcommittee on Quality Assurance and Quality Control have remained particularly active. The NRC's participation was requested and funded by the state of California and the U.S. Department of the Interior beginning in early 1985 and is scheduled to end in March 1990.

The structure of the SJVDP, with these many layers of advisors and participants, provides a great breadth of expertise and interests in the planning process and is an example of the type of interagency coordination necessary to deal with complex environmental problems. It also, however, makes the SJVDP cumbersome and, given the passion inherent in water politics in California, often controversial. Along with their assigned responsibilities for research and planning, the staff of the SJVDP have been put in the unenviable position of intermediary among many powerful interests. It can be quite challenging to balance the demands of science with the needs of politics. As an example, it has been extremely difficult for the SJVDP to assess the full range of options available to respond to the irrigation-related problems when the program staff has been instructed to address only certain in-valley solutions. This boundary on the SJVDP's activities limits the potential effectiveness of the planning process and imposes a short-sighted view of the causes and consequences of irrigation-induced water quality problems.

THE NATIONAL IRRIGATION WATER QUALITY PROGRAM

As mentioned earlier, the events at Kesterson NWR alerted the nation to the potential for irrigation-induced water quality problems. One response to this new awareness was the SJVDP. In late 1985, however, a further response was initiated when the U.S. Department of the Interior created the National Irrigation Water Quality Program (NIWQP). This program committed the department to a systematic review of other areas in the West where such problems might arise, including irrigation and drainage facilities, national wildlife refuges, and other sites managed by the U.S. Department of the Interior where migratory birds or endangered species receive irrigation water.

The National Irrigation Water Quality Program seeks to identify and address other potential problem sites through a five-step process (Figure

Site Identification	Reconnaissance investigations	Detailed Studies	Planning	Remediation
				Kesterson Reservoir, CA
		San Joaquin Valley, CA		(Planning to be completed by end of 1990)
		Salton Sea, CA Tulare Lake, CA Stillwater NWR, NV Middle Green River, UT Kendrick Project, WY	(Detailed studies to be completed at end of 1990)	
		Lower Colorado River, AZ/CA Sun River, MT Milk River, MT Laguna Atascosa, TX	(Long-term monitoring)	
	Upper Sacramento River, CA Klamath Basin, CA/OR Gunnison River, CO Pine River, CO Middle Arkansas, CO/KS American Falls Reservoir, ID Bosque del Apache NWR, NM Malheur NWR, OR Angostura Unit, SD Belle Fourche Project, SD Riverton Unit, WY	(Reconnaissance investigations to be completed at end of 1989)		

FIGURE 1.4 The National Irrigation Water Quality Program's five-step process.
SOURCE: Courtesy of the U.S. Department of the Interior.

1.4). Step 1, site identification, includes an ongoing examination of existing information to determine which sites are most likely to have irrigation-induced contamination problems. To date, a comprehensive survey of about 600 irrigation projects and major wildlife areas is nearing completion, and 22 sites in 13 states have been identified as having a high potential for such problems. Potential problem sites identified from this step progress to step 2, reconnaissance investigations. These investigations include field sampling studies to obtain basic data on potentially toxic elements in the water, sediment, plants, fish, and waterfowl. Reconnaissance investigations have been completed at 11 of the original 22 sites.

Sites showing significant signs of contamination problems progress to step 3, detailed studies. These more in-depth field investigations gather data and interpret information necessary to identify the sources of the problems and evaluate remediation alternatives. Of the 11 sites for which reconnaissance investigations have been completed as of spring 1989, 7 were determined to have problems warranting continued study. Two detailed studies are complete; five detailed studies are under way and are expected

The Belle Fourche Project, South Dakota, serves more than 57,000 acres of farmland. This site underwent a reconnaissance-level investigation under the U.S. Department of the Interior's National Irrigation Water Quality Program. No significant problems were identified, but the site will be monitored over the long term to ensure that fish and wildlife are protected from possible irrigation-related problems.
CREDIT: U.S. Bureau of Reclamation, L. C. Axthelm.

to be complete by the end of 1990. The Committee on Irrigation-Induced Water Quality Problems has been involved in oversight activities relating to the NIWQP. The committee has reviewed draft work plans for various reconnaissance and detailed studies, participated in mid-course meetings with the field staff, and reviewed draft reports.

No sites identified through the NIWQP process have progressed to the final steps: step 4, planning, and step 5, remediation. However, looking comprehensively at the U.S. Department of the Interior's activities related to irrigation-induced contamination, two sites are in these final stages. Step 4, planning, has been completed at one site, Kesterson NWR, and is under way at another via the SJVDP. The Kesterson site is the only site currently undergoing remediation.

Funding for the NIWQP's activities thus far (Table 1.2) has been provided cooperatively in the budgets of the USBR, USGS, USFWS, and the Bureau of Indian Affairs. Also, the Bureau of Land Management has provided some funding in the past. Funding for the Kesterson NWR

TABLE 1.2 Appropriated Funds, National Irrigation Water Quality
Program (in millions of dollars)

| Activity | Fiscal Year | | | | | |
	1985	1986	1987	1988	1989	1990 (est.)
Westwide investigations	--	1.0	0.9	3.6	4.2	2.8
Kesterson cleanup	0.5	3.7	9.6	18.4	10.9	3.7
San Joaquin Valley Drainage Program	7.5	9.6	7.9	11.2	13.0	--
Total	8.0	14.3	18.4	33.2	28.1	6.5

SOURCE: U.S. Department of the Interior.

cleanup and the SJVDP is provided in the USBR budget. The organization
of the NIWQP shows interagency cooperation and outside input (Figure
1.5). The field teams conducting research at the reconnaissance and detailed
studies sites are generally composed of representatives of the different
federal funding agencies, as well as some state and local agencies. As the
program continues in operation and as more sites enter the planning and
remediation stages, the USBR expects to have an increasingly important
role. The NIWQP does not have a set end date, and discussions regarding
its continued importance for site identification and long-term monitoring
will ultimately need to be addressed.

FUTURE IRRIGATION AND DRAINAGE ISSUES

It would be a serious mistake to view the damage caused by selenium
at Kesterson NWR as an isolated incident. Other sites have already been
identified that show potential contamination problems and warrant more
extensive research, and the search for similar problems is continuing (Deason, 1989). Although this report, and the U.S. Department of the Interior's
ongoing efforts, focus on problems that originate from public projects, it
should be remembered that the same potential for problems exists for
private irrigation projects as well. Similarly, although this report focuses
on naturally occurring trace elements, the potential for problems related to
manufactured contaminants should also be given serious attention.

What happened at Kesterson NWR provides a clear illustration of
the long-known fact that irrigation projects without adequate outlets for
drainage create unacceptable levels of salinity. The unexpected part of

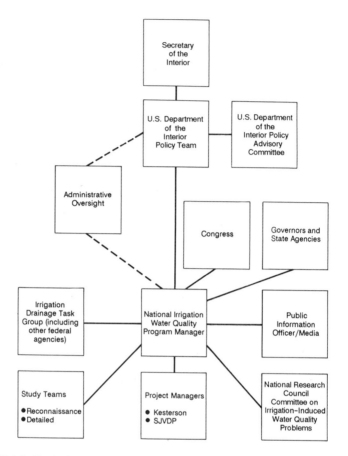

FIGURE 1.5   Participants in the National Irrigation Water Quality Program.
SOURCE: Courtesy of the U.S. Department of the Interior.

the scenario was that—given the right soils and geology and a setting where water accumulates in holding ponds or reservoirs—drainage water can contain trace elements that can accumulate to toxic levels and cause serious harm to the biota. This is a type of problem that the nation must be better prepared to address.

REFERENCES

California Department of Water Resources. 1987. California Water: Looking to the Future. Bulletin 160-87.

California State Department of Public Works, Division of Water Resources. 1932. Bulletin of the Great Central Valley Project of the State Water Plan of California. California State Printing Office, Sacramento, California.

Deason, J. P. 1989. Irrigation-induced contamination: How real a problem? Journal of Irrigation and Drainage Engineering 115, 9-20.

Dudek, D. J., and G. L. Horner. 1981. Integrated Physical-Economic Resource Analysis: A Case Study of the San Joaquin Valley. Final Report to the Environmental Protection Agency. U.S. Department of Agriculture, Agricultural Research Service. Robert Kerr Environmental Research Laboratory, Ada, Oklahoma.

El-Ashry, M. T., and D. C. Gibbons. 1986. Troubled Waters: New Policies for Managing Water in the American West. Study 6. World Resources Institute, Washington, D.C. October.

Frederick, K. D., and J. C. Hanson. 1984. Water for Western Agriculture. Resources for the Future, Washington, D.C.

Hilgard, E. W. 1886. Irrigation and Alkali in India. College of Agriculture, University of California, Report to the President of the University, Bulletin No. 86. California State Printing Office, Sacramento, California, pp. 34-35.

Letey, J., C. Roberts, M. Penberth, and C. Vasek. 1986. An Agricultural Dilemma: Drainage Water and Toxics Disposal in the San Joaquin Valley. Special Publication 3319. Agricultural Experiment Station. University of California, Riverside. Division of Agriculture and Natural Resources.

Lohman, L. C., J. G. Milliken, W. S. Dorn, and K. E. Tuccy. 1988. Estimating Economic Impacts of Salinity of the Colorado River. Prepared for the U.S. Bureau of Reclamation, Water Quality Office, Denver, Colorado.

Ogden, G. R. 1988. Agricultural Land Use and Wildlife in the San Joaquin Valley, 1769-1930: An Overview. SOLO Heritage Research, Report prepared for the San Joaquin Valley Drainage Program, 2800 Cottage Way, Rm. W-2143, Sacramento, California.

Ohlendorf, H. M. 1984. The biologic system. Pp. 8-15 in U.S. Bureau of Reclamation and Ecological Analysis. Proceedings of a research meeting on toxicity problems at Kesterson Reservoir, California. U.S. Bureau of Reclamation, Mid-Pacific Region, Sacramento, California.

Ohlendorf, H. M. 1989. Bioaccumulation and effects of selenium in wildlife, 1989. Pp. 133-177 in Selenium in Agriculture and the Environment. L. W. Jacobs, ed. SSSA Special Publication No. 23. American Society of Agronomy, Inc., Madison, Wisconsin.

Peterson, D. A., W. E. Jones, and A. G. Morton. 1988. Reconnaissance Investigation of Water Quality, Bottom Sediment, and Biota Associated with Irrigation Drainage in the Kendrick Reclamation Project Area, Wyoming, 1986-87. U.S. Geological Survey, Water Resources Investigations Report 88-401. U.S. Geological Survey, Denver, Colorado.

Presser, T. S., and I. Barnes. 1984. Selenium Concentration in the Waters Tributary to and in the Vicinity of the Kesterson National Wildlife Refuge, Fresno and Merced Counties, California. U.S. Geological Survey, Water Resources Investigations Report 84-4122. U.S. Geological Survey, Federal Center, Denver, Colorado.

Presser, T., and H. M. Ohlendorf. 1987. Biogeochemical cycling of selenium in the San Joaquin Valley, California, USA. Environmental Management 11, 805-821.

San Joaquin Valley Drainage Program (SJVDP). 1987a. Developing Options: An Overview of Efforts to Solve Agricultural Drainage and Drainage-Related Problems in the San Joaquin Valley. San Joaquin Valley Drainage Program, 2800 Cottage Way, Rm. W-2143, Sacramento, California.

San Joaquin Valley Drainage Program (SJVDP). 1987b. Prospectus. San Joaquin Valley Drainage Program, 2800 Cottage Way, Rm. W-2143, Sacramento, California.

Stephens, D. W., B. Waddell, and J. Miller. 1988. Reconnaissance Investigation of Water Quality, Bottom Sediment, and Biota Associated with Irrigation Drainage in the Middle Green River Basin, Utah, 1986-87. U.S. Geological Survey, Water Resources Investigations Report 88-401. U.S. Geological Survey, Denver, Colorado.

U.S. Bureau of Reclamation. 1984. Water, Land, and Related Data. Summary Statistics. Vol. 1. USBR, Washington, D.C., p. 6.

U.S. Environmental Protection Agency. 1974. Evaluation of Salinity Created by Irrigation Return Flows. U.S. Environmental Protection Agency, Washington, D.C., p. 36.

U.S. Geological Survey. 1983. National Water Summary. U.S. Government Printing Office, Washington, D.C.

van Schilfgaarde, J., and J. D. Rhoades. 1984. Coping with salinity. Pp. 157-179 in Water Scarcity: Impacts on Western Agriculture. E. A. Engelbert and A. F. Schearing, eds. University of California Press, Berkeley, California.

2
Understanding the Scientific Dimensions of an Environmental Problem

Decisionmakers must have a basic understanding of the general processes by which irrigation degrades water quality before they can resolve irrigation-induced problems, and this understanding needs to encompass both scientific and institutional dimensions. This chapter briefly reviews some of the hydrological, chemical, geological, ecological, and other physical factors that affect and are affected by irrigation. Understanding that these factors set the stage for the development of problems is critical to any attempt to select potential solutions, because no solution can be successful unless it reflects some knowledge of the underlying natural processes at work. The issues highlighted here are discussed extensively in other publications (e.g., Letey et al., 1986; SJVDP, 1987; USCID, 1986). Chapter 3 examines the relevant institutional issues.

HOW IRRIGATION DRAINAGE ALTERS WATER QUALITY

Irrigation, simply defined, is the act of supplying land with water by artificial means. Like other uses of water, irrigation degrades water quality for some later users, particularly in arid climates. Irrigation also can lead to an increase in soil salinity. The processes by which these changes occur are natural, but they can be significantly accelerated under irrigation because of the increased quantities of water involved (Brady, 1974). Substantially less natural leaching occurs in arid and semiarid regions than in humid areas because less water is available; thus the changes caused by irrigation can be more pronounced.

Like other uses of water, irrigation can degrade water quality. This happens because all irrigation water contains dissolved salts, and these salts are left behind as the water evaporates from the soil surface or is taken up by plants and returned to the atmosphere. If irrigation is to be maintained, adequate water must move down through the soil profile to reduce the concentration of dissolved material in the root zone. If irrigation is a desired use of water, then its waste waters must be treated and/or disposal provided for.
CREDIT: U.S. Bureau of Reclamation, J. C. Dahilig.

The potential for water quality degradation and salinity problems arising from irrigation exists because all water contains dissolved salts. The concentration of these salts, however, varies considerably depending on the origin of the water. Once irrigation water has been applied to a field, it moves away from the point of application by various routes. Some water evaporates from the soil surface, but much more is taken up by plants and returned to the atmosphere through plant leaves. As this transpiration continues, the salts originally dissolved in the irrigation water are left behind. These mineral salts remain in the soil unless sufficient quantities of water are applied to leach out the salts and carry them below the root zone. Any water remaining in the root zone has a higher concentration of dissolved salts (salinity) than the originally applied irrigation water had. If the salinity in the root zone increases too much, plants grow more slowly, salt-sensitive plants die, and agriculture in the area suffers.

Adequate drainage—whether natural or provided through installation of drainage systems—is a necessity to maintain irrigated agriculture over time. Without leaching, the concentration of salts dispersed in soil solutions continues to increase and can become sufficiently high that it prevents crops from absorbing water. Without drainage to remove the leaching water, the water table will rise. The end result is a waterlogged, saline soil. Other factors can complicate the picture by either slowing or hastening the fundamental trend, but they do not stop it.

Irrigated agriculture will always be a short-lived enterprise unless the salts accumulating in the root zone are leached out. In most unaltered (by humans) ecosystems, the most common path for soluble salt removal is through the natural drainage system (e.g., rivers and creeks) to the ocean. Over geologic time, the ocean is the ultimate sink for all dissolved salts in the surface drainage system. Not all areas drain to the sea in a human time frame, however. Drainage water can and does collect in closed basins. Examples include the Dead Sea on the Jordan-Israel border, the Salton Sea in southern California, and the Great Salt Lake in Utah, as well as the reservoirs at both the Stillwater Wildlife Management area in Nevada and Kesterson National Wildlife Refuge (NWR) in California.

As the names of some of these areas suggest, these natural or human-made low points accumulate both water and salts. The water also leads to the growth of riparian vegetation, and this attracts waterfowl and other wildlife. When such enclosed water bodies are used to dispose of irrigation drainage water, they may, through evaporation and other processes, become saline quite quickly and can ultimately lose their capacity to support biological productivity and diversity. The accumulation of trace elements (some of which are toxic in low concentrations) and of agricultural pollutants, such as pesticides or nitrates and phosphates from fertilizers, can accelerate the deterioration of water quality, sometimes with disastrous results.

As irrigation waters are concentrated in the soil, some of the dissolved salts precipitate and form solid-phase minerals; thus the minerals gypsum ($CaSO_4 \cdot 2H_2O$) and calcium carbonate ($CaCO_3$) often accumulate in the solid phase, becoming part of the soil. In other circumstances, salts may be dissolved from the soil, a process that can lead to an increased concentration of dissolved salts in the soil water. Highly saline drainage waters may also displace good-quality ground water.

The leaching of soluble minerals from the soil and the displacement of ground water are natural processes. Irrigation accelerates both processes. Any water (whether from rainfall or irrigation) applied to the land in excess of the evaporative demand passes down through the root zone and becomes part of the local ground water. A rising ground water table, in turn, increases local drainage flow. (A "mound" of water develops under the irrigation project.) On its subsurface path toward an outlet and ultimate disposal or dispersal, the drainage water displaces older ground water; frequently, this ground water contains dissolved salts of geologic origin. Both drainage and displaced water ultimately flow via the surface or subsurface drainage system and eventually end up in the ocean. When the drainage process is interrupted by a closed basin (such as in Kesterson NWR), the waters become trapped and can form "salt" lakes.

As the amount of land irrigated in the arid West increases, stream salt loadings in areas of irrigation will also increase. Thus, the quality of water is degraded as it moves downstream through a watershed in an arid climate. An illustration may help to clarify this point. The total dissolved solids concentration (TDS) in the upper reaches of the Colorado River is generally less than 200 milligrams per liter (mg/l); the TDS of the lower reaches, where the river enters Mexico, typically is around 800 to 900 mg/l. Over one-third of this increased salt load is contributed by the irrigated areas in the Colorado River basin (Jonez, 1983). Major salinity control programs have been undertaken (cf. P.L. 93-320) to obtain a salinity level agreed upon by treaty with Mexico, the last user on the river.

In the Grand River valley of Colorado, water is diverted from the Colorado River for irrigation. Some of it is used consumptively, and some returns to the river, but a substantial part (20 percent) infiltrates into the soil and displaces ground water from the underlying salt-rich substrates. This displaced saline ground water then flows into the river, increasing the salt load. Water from the same river is again diverted for irrigation in the Imperial and Coachella Valleys in California. Irrigation drainage water from these areas then carries the salts leached out of the soils to the Salton Sea.

In many areas, natural drainage rates are adequate to meet the needs of irrigated agriculture. In other locales, the rates are too slow, and human-made drainage systems—such as underground collector tubes or tile drains, open ditches, or pumped wells—are added. Whatever their engineering configuration, their purpose is to collect drainage water, sometimes of high salinity, for disposal. The distinction between drainage water from a human-made collector system and drainage water from natural processes can raise important institutional issues and can affect capital costs. Conceptually, however, there is no difference between them: the drainage water must be removed to avoid waterlogging and salinization.

The dominant dissolved salt species involved in these processes include the carbonates, bicarbonates, sulfates, and chlorides of sodium, calcium, and magnesium. The adverse effects of these salts have long been recognized, and considerable efforts have been expended in learning how to minimize them. Past experience with elements present in minor or trace amounts indicated that, in most instances, their concentrations were low enough that adverse effects were of little concern. However, recent investigations have shown potential, serious impacts, especially for the trace elements selenium, molybdenum, and arsenic (Deason, 1989).

These elements were not carried in by irrigation water in most cases but instead originated from in situ dissolving of geological materials. This situation has added a new dimension to the problem of irrigation water management. Drainage must now be managed not only to reduce salt accumulation in the root zone and salt disposal in streams, but also to limit the toxic effects of selected trace elements contributed by the local geology. Furthermore, as noted earlier, agricultural drainage waters often contain other contaminants (e.g., nitrates, pesticides, and soluble constituents). Nitrate, for example, is a particularly mobile component, is easily leached, and moves readily with water. It has been identified as a common cause of ground water contamination beneath agricultural lands in California and elsewhere (Freeze and Cherry, 1979).

If irrigated agriculture is to be maintained, adequate water must move down through the soil profile to reduce the concentration of solutes (dissolved material) in the root zone so that they do not exceed the level that can be tolerated by the crops. Although the quantity of this flux can be managed, the removal of excess salts is mandatory. Thus **irrigated agriculture over time cannot avoid causing an adverse offsite effect. This effect must be acknowledged: it can be minimized, internalized, or rejected, but it cannot be ignored. If irrigation is a desired use of water, then its waste waters must be treated and/or disposal provided for.**

HYDROLOGY AND SOILS

The problems in the San Joaquin Valley—and the selenium contamination at Kesterson NWR—vividly illustrate the relationship between the physical environment and irrigation-induced water quality problems. Two critical preconditions that set the stage in this case, and that play a similarly fundamental role in these kinds of problems elsewhere, are hydrology and soil composition. The soils on the west side of the San Joaquin Valley are primarily derived from marine sedimentary rocks in the Coast Range. These soils contain materials commonly found in areas of salt water deposition. The sediments are fine-textured, and they contain impermeable clay layers and elevated levels of trace elements (e.g., chromium, arsenic, and boron) that are toxic at low concentrations.

Soils on the east side of the San Joaquin Valley are derived from granitic parent material of the Sierra Nevada mountains to the east. These soils are coarser-textured, contain little salt, and have fewer water-restricting clay layers. Consequently, waters on the east side contain much lower concentrations of dissolved salts (Letey et al., 1986).

The confining clay layers underlying the valley's west side inhibit deep infiltration of the irrigation waters. Thus, as irrigation water was introduced from outside the valley, the level of the prevailing water table rose. A high, saline water table extending up into the root zone developed. High water tables reduce crop productivity and increase soil management problems. Many farmers have installed subsurface drain tubes buried 6 to 10 ft deep, to supplement the natural drainage by collecting and conducting the leachates out of waterlogged fields. The waters are then collected in sumps and either pumped into discharge channels or conveyed to them by gravity. These waters eventually work their way into the regional drainage system.

GEOLOGY AND GEOCHEMISTRY

Selenium is found in a variety of geologic formations. The marine shales in California, South Dakota, and other western states, coal from West Virginia and Kentucky, and volcanic formations in Hawaii all provide high selenium concentrations. Selenium normally enters the biosphere by natural weathering from the rocks that contain it. Areas of low and high endemic selenium intake in humans and livestock have been identified around the world. Western Oregon, parts of the midwestern United States, most of New Zealand, and several areas of China generally have low or very low soil levels of selenium, which may lead to low intakes in humans and animals. Other areas of China, parts of Venezuela, and some localities in the Great Plains region of the United States have high or very high soil selenium levels with the potential for excess intakes (Burk, 1984).

The selenium problems at Kesterson NWR resulted from a combination of natural geologic factors and human influences. The San Joaquin Valley is a structural trough or valley lying between the Sierra Nevada mountains on the east and the Coast Range on the west. As noted, the soils in the basin trough were developed from a mix of geologic materials derived from both ranges, but predominantly from the Sierra Nevada. The deposits on the west side of the trough were formed by ephemeral and intermittent streams coming out of the Coast Range.

The Coast Range shale deposits are of marine origin and contain a high level of soluble salts and pyritic material. Selenium and seleniferous salts are commonly associated with pyritic materials. In contrast, the igneous rocks of the Sierra Nevada tend to form soils low in soluble salts and low in pyrite and selenium-bearing minerals. Both geologic sources, however, contribute significant amounts of other trace elements, such as arsenic, boron, and molybdenum (Deverel and Millard, 1988).

Ground water moving downgradient toward the valley carries with it soluble salts and, specifically, selenium. In time, transpiration and evaporation cause salts to accumulate in the trough. Much of the variation in salinity and selenium found in the shallow ground water or in the local soils today is the result of natural processes and the impact of irrigation. For example, soils that have been irrigated longer tend to have lost most of their soluble selenium and other soluble salts, whereas in more recently irrigated soils, present-day ground water salinity is closely correlated with soil salinity (Deverel and Gallanthine, 1988).

Very likely, the San Joaquin Valley's problems with selenium would never have surfaced had it not been for human intervention. Natural drainage from the valley was provided by the San Joaquin River system, and dissolved salts, including selenium, were transported by this system through to the delta and thence to the ocean. Introduction of irrigation, with water imported from outside the valley, led to the need for additional drainage capacity. It also mobilized the salts and selenium stored in the soil profile.

Although the U.S. Bureau of Reclamation (USBR) anticipated problems associated with the management of saline soils and drainage water in the San Joaquin Valley and made plans to mitigate them, it did not anticipate the selenium problem; neither the USBR nor any other group anticipated that selenium could or would be a problem until it was actually encountered in the drainage water. Selenium was not recognized as a problem associated with the management of saline soils and drain water until recently (Fujii et al., 1987). The problem stems from the cycling of selenium induced largely by irrigation, collection of drainage water in a master drain, delivery and storage in a closed basin (Kesterson NWR), concentration by evaporation, accumulation by biota, and transfer up the trophic chain. Figure 2.1 shows in a general way the biogeochemical cycling of selenium from its primary source (igneous extrusions and volcanic gases) through pathways to aquatic life, man, and animals.

The source of the selenium problem in the Kesterson NWR begins with the chemical form of the selenium that occurs in soils and in the parent materials. The parent materials for most of the seleniferous soils in the western United States, including those in the Kesterson region, are Cretaceous shales (Boon, 1989). Compared to igneous and other sedimentary rocks, the shales of Cretaceous age are elevated in selenium. For example, whereas the average concentration of selenium (Se) in the earth's crust is approximately 0.09 mg Se $\cdot$ kg^{-1}, Cretaceous Pierre and related shales average 2 mg Se $\cdot$ kg^{-1} and may contain as much as a few hundred mg Se $\cdot$ kg^{-1} (Lakin, 1972). Soils developed from these parent materials commonly contain from 1 to 10 mg Se $\cdot$ kg^{-1}, compared to a mean for the entire western United States of 0.23 mg Se $\cdot$ kg^{-1} (Shacklette and Boerngen, 1984). Where soils are alkaline, selenium occurs mainly in

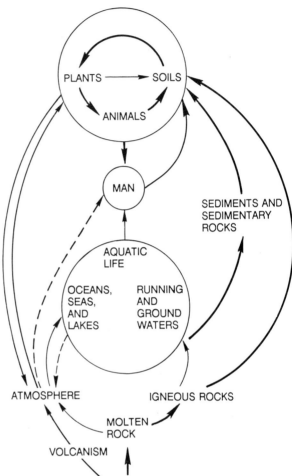

FIGURE 2.1 Cycling of selenium in nature.
SOURCE: National Research Council, 1976.

the selenate (+6) form. Owing to its stability at alkaline pH values, its high solubility, and its ready availability to plants, selenate is considered to be the most dangerous chemical form of selenium as far as potential environmental problems are concerned.

The chemistry of selenium resembles that of sulfur (S). Like sulfur, selenium has four oxidation states: −2, 0, +4, and +6. The solubility and chemical form of selenium in soil solutions and surface waters depend mainly on the pH and the redox condition of the system. In reducing environments (waterlogged and/or flooded conditions), selenium exists in the −2 (selenide) or 0 (elemental) oxidation state. Selenides and elemental selenium are very insoluble in water and as such quite inert and essentially unavailable to biota (Elrashidi et al., 1989).

In aerated systems, selenium occurs in either the +4 or +6 oxidation state, depending mainly on the pH of the system. At high redox potentials (>400 millivolts) and under alkaline conditions, the +6 form of selenium as selenate ion (SeO_4^{-2}) is the dominant dissolved species. At moderate oxidative potentials (100 to 400 millivolts) and near neutral to slightly alkaline conditions, the selenite species (SeO_3^{-2}) is dominant, whereas under acid conditions (pH ~3 to 7), the biselenite ($HSeO_3^-$) species dominates.

Selenium is an element essential for animal nutrition, but the range between dietary requirements and toxic levels is quite narrow. In general, dietary requirements for most animals range from 0.05 to 0.3 mg Se • kg^{-1}, while a dietary concentration of 2 mg Se • kg^{-1} on a continuing basis is suggested as a maximum tolerable level for all species (National Research Council, 1980). The availability of selenium to biota depends largely on its chemical form and competitive interactions among similar constituents (i.e., sulfate, arsenate, and so on). In humid areas where parent materials are high in selenium, slightly soluble selenite and biselenite oxyhydroxides of iron and manganese are likely to form (Elrashidi et al., 1989). Because of the sparingly soluble nature of the selenite forms of selenium, plants grown on soils in these regions will not contain levels of selenium that will produce forage with levels potentially harmful to animals. However, they should produce vegetation containing adequate selenium to protect wildlife and domestic animals from selenium deficiency. In humid regions where parent materials are low in selenium, plants produced are likely to contain insufficient selenium, and deficiencies can result.

In well-drained, arid and semiarid regions where parent materials are high in selenium, selenate and organic forms commonly dominate. The selenate salts are highly soluble in water and readily available to biota. Consequently, these areas are most likely to produce terrestrial vegetation containing potentially toxic levels of selenium. Likewise in poorly drained, periodically flooded areas where parent materials are high in selenium (e.g., Kesterson NWR) under alkaline conditions, both terrestrial and aquatic vegetation may accumulate sufficient selenium to harm aquatic organisms, waterfowl, and wildlife.

The selenium distribution in soils on the west side of the San Joaquin Valley is influenced by landscape, topography, evaporation, and leaching characteristics. Not surprisingly, soils located near selenium-containing geologic materials have higher concentrations of selenium in the upper soil horizons. Where the parent material source is more distant, weathering and leaching result in the selenium being found in the subsoil. Selenium

The value of agriculture is no less important to the nation today than in the past; however, the value of other natural resources has increased in the public's perception. Efforts to respond to irrigation-induced water quality problems need to recognize the increased importance of these other environmental values. The availability of adequate fish and wildlife habitat, as illustrated here along the Colorado River, is a critical consideration. CREDIT: U.S. Bureau of Reclamation, E. E. Hertzog.

thus exists in shallow ground water at concentrations ranging from levels too low for detection to levels of several hundred micrograms per liter.

FISH AND WILDLIFE CONSIDERATIONS

Another important scientific consideration for decisionmakers studying irrigation-related contamination is fish and wildlife habitat. Public concern for the quality of the habitat provided at Kesterson NWR was the major force motivating cleanup efforts at that problem site and is but one example of society's increased attention to non-economic environmental values.

Once again, the California example is illustrative. The Central Valley of California once contained some of the finest bird and anadromous fish habitats in the world. As the valley was developed and lands were converted to agricultural use, fish and wildlife resources declined (Figure 2.2). Today

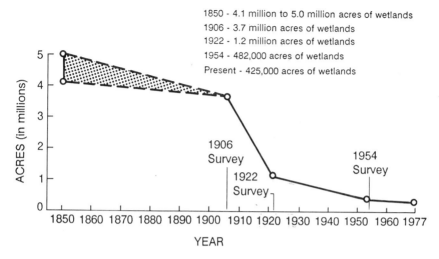

FIGURE 2.2 Wetland losses in California, 1850 to 1977. Note: Estimates prior to 1900 range from 4.1 million to 5 million acres.
SOURCE: SJVDP, 1987.

only 300,000 to 425,000 acres of wetlands remain out of an estimated 4 million. In addition, an historic 6000 miles of productive stream and river habitat have been reduced by about 85 percent, to only 950 miles, as a result of the construction of dams and other major water developments (U.S. Fish and Wildlife Service, 1982a).

Reduction of productive habitats has resulted in corresponding reductions of fish and wildlife populations. A large number of species of migratory birds, including waterfowl, shore birds, waders, raptors, and passerines, winter in or pass through the Central Valley. About 60 percent of the waterfowl population of the Pacific Flyway, including the entire population of the endangered Aleutian Canada Goose, use the remaining valley wetland habitat (U.S. Fish and Wildlife Service, 1982b). The Northern American Waterfowl Management Plan, adopted in 1986 by Canada and the United States, recognized the importance of wetland habitat for wintering flyway populations and established a goal of improving the quality of all publicly managed habitat areas (U.S. Fish and Wildlife Service, 1986).

Agriculture has long been considered the primary water user in the West and has rights to the best-quality water. Many wildlife refuges in the arid West are, in essence, terminal points for irrigation drainage schemes. These areas often are located in closed basins with no outlet to the sea, and so water quality problems can become severe. In all cases, the reduction in stream flow and the deteriorating quality of water have been stressful for fish and wildlife.

The discovery of selenium in these terminal points—Kesterson NWR is but one example, albeit the first—is of particular concern because of (1) selenium's effect on reproductive capacity, (2) its developmental toxicity, and (3) its ability to bring about mortality for selected waterfowl. These harmful effects indicate the hazards of relying on irrigation drainage water as a source of water for wildlife refuges. Other elements such as arsenic, cadmium, lead, chromium, boron, mercury, and molybdenum also are found in selected drainage waters. Significantly high concentrations of any of these elements in western wildlife refuges can be deleterious to living things. Plant life, for example, is particularly sensitive to boron.

For the San Joaquin Valley, the decision to build the upper part of the San Luis Drain before building the lower part (the outlet) set an unexpected series of events in motion. As drainage waters were conveyed to the ponds in Kesterson NWR and evaporated, salts accumulated as expected. What was unanticipated was the buildup of high concentrations of selenium and its consequent bioconcentration, which has had severe impacts on waterfowl and fish. These effects, in turn, called attention to other problems, such as the high levels of boron in the drainage waters, and also sparked investigations looking for similar problems elsewhere in the West.

PUBLIC HEALTH CONSIDERATIONS

Irrigation drainage waters often contain elevated concentrations of many elements of geologic origin, as well as agricultural chemicals. When the presence of elements of concern results in potential direct or indirect exposure of humans, a public health concern may arise. To date, the most frequently encountered public health concern from irrigation in the arid West has been caused by elevated selenium concentrations, and therefore its implications are discussed here as an example. Selenium is an essential element necessary to human and animal health, but it has the potential to cause toxicity at elevated levels. The margin of safety between levels considered essential and levels associated with toxicity is small.

Natural sources of selenium have been known to cause toxicity in free-living animal and human populations in regions around the world. In areas of China and South Dakota, for example, "alkali disease" and "blind staggers" (chronic and acute forms of animal selenium toxicity, respectively) have been seen in animals grazing on seleniferous forage (Klasing and Schenker, 1988). Blind staggers occurs in animals that consume selenium-accumulator plants over a period of weeks or months. The affected animals have impaired vision, and they wander, stagger, and finally succumb to respiratory failure (Rosenfeld and Beath, 1964).

Selenosis in humans is characterized by hair and nail changes, gastrointestinal discomfort and diarrhea, skin abnormalities, garlic breath, nausea, fatigue, and irritability. No human deaths clearly attributable to selenium toxicity from chronic exposure have ever been reported, although there have been cases of acute selenium poisoning (Longnecker, 1989). Because deficiency and toxicity syndromes are relatively rare in humans, the effects of chronic low or high selenium intakes in humans have not been clearly defined (Klasing and Schenker, 1988). An episode of human selenium toxicosis was observed in a region of China where environmental selenium was unusually high and where human exposures were increased because of drought conditions (Levander, 1986).

As the San Joaquin Valley experience illustrates, human activities can hasten the entry of selenium into the biosphere. Irrigation is not the only mechanism: for instance, some coals produce a seleniferous fly ash that, if improperly disposed of, can release selenium to enter the food chain. In some South Dakota rivers, erosion and damming have contributed to elevated selenium levels in the water. Similarly, irrigation-induced selenium in water also has contributed to abnormally high selenium levels in wildlife in Utah. Concern for public health surfaces because hunters and fishermen may ingest fish and wildlife containing elevated concentrations of selenium.

The average American diet contains a safe and adequate selenium intake, 50 to 200 micrograms per day (μg/day) (National Research Council, 1980). Meats, especially liver and kidney, dairy products, eggs, certain seafoods, and wheat products contribute most of the selenium. Selenium intake depends on the amount of these foods consumed and their selenium concentration, which varies by region. In general, it appears that healthy adults are unlikely to suffer from selenium deficiency if their daily intake is greater than 50 μg, and they are unlikely to suffer from selenium toxicity if their daily intake is less than 5 μg per kilogram of body weight (or 350 μg/day for a person weighing 70 kg) (Olson, 1986).

Studies initiated on behalf of the San Joaquin Valley Drainage Program on human health concerns associated with selenium in or near the Kesterson Reservoir indicated that there was no basis for serious alarm in that region (Klasing and Pilch, 1988). That does not mean, however, that there is no reason for further study of selenium uptake into food plants from irrigation water in other areas. For example, in a survey of 107 irrigation and 44 livestock wells in the southern California Coast Range, selenium levels were found to be above the drinking water standard (10 μg/l) in 26 wells; the irrigation water standard (20 μg/l) was exceeded in 11 wells (Oster et al., 1988). Other preliminary studies also have shown elevated levels of selenium in some food products, but not to levels that warrant ameliorative action. Thus the evidence to date indicates somewhat elevated levels of selenium in some irrigation waters, with consequent elevation in some food crops or animal products; however, to date the probability of an adverse effect on the general population is remote. The relationship between selenium in well waters and geological mapping units is clear enough that reasonable predictions are feasible without excessive monitoring (Tracy et al., 1989).

In more general terms, any actions taken to address the agricultural drainage problem in the San Joaquin Valley (or elsewhere) will result in changes in the distribution, concentration, and possibly the types of potentially hazardous contaminants to which people are exposed. Thus any program to evaluate the feasibility and desirability of various actions to resolve the problems of agricultural drainage should explicitly address the public health concerns that might be raised by such actions. The public health component of these evaluations should include the following steps:

1. An analysis of potential changes in the physical, chemical, and biological transport and fate of contaminants resulting from a proposed action.

2. An analysis of the potential intensity and extent of human exposure resulting from those actions. This exposure assessment should consider total exposure, including exposure through drinking water, air, foodstuffs, and other possible routes.

3. An analysis of possible health effects that might result from the exposures identified in step 2 above. To the extent feasible, these assessments should consider synergistic and antagonistic effects among the contaminants, and other possible health risks that exposed populations might face.

CONCLUSIONS

Irrigated agriculture remains the most significant water user in the West. Throughout the West, however, there is increasing pressure on a diminishing and deteriorating water resource from numerous competing interests (e.g., urbanization). With this competition comes an increasing need, real and perceived, to find solutions to water quality problems acceptable not only to the irrigation interests but also to other parties. The historic conversion of wetlands and wildlife habitats to agricultural and other uses compounds the need to protect the remaining natural areas and to ensure an uncontaminated water supply for state and federal refuges and other wetlands.

The discovery of selenium poisoning in Kesterson NWR raises the question of whether similar problems are occurring elsewhere. The answer is clearly affirmative. The geohydrology of the West is such that the processes that caused the accumulation of selenium in the San Joaquin Valley are likely to play a similar role at other locations. The events that have happened there over the past few years not only have heightened the nation's awareness of such problems, but also have added a sense of urgency to the search for solutions.

The primary problem associated with irrigation traditionally has been salinity and how to dispose of drainage water at minimal cost to the irrigator. Now, however, there is an added dimension: how to protect downstream and offsite users from the adverse effects caused by selenium and other trace element contaminants. The events in California's San Joaquin Valley and Kesterson NWR have caused some people to challenge past assumptions that the benefits of irrigation always outweigh the costs. As the demand for water increases, these problems will become more acute.

REFERENCES

Boon, D. Y. 1989. Potential selenium problems in Great Plains soils. Pp. 107-121 in Selenium in Agriculture and the Environment. Special Publ. No. 23. L. W. Jacobs, ed. American Society of Agronomy, Inc., Madison, Wisconsin.

Brady, N. C. 1974. The Nature and Properties of Soils. 8th Ed. MacMillan, New York.

Burk, R. F. 1984. Selenium. Pp. 519-527 in Present Knowledge in Nutrition. 5th Ed. R. E. Olson, chairman. The Nutrition Foundation, Washington, D.C.

Deason, J. P. 1989. Irrigation-induced contamination: How real a problem? Journal of Irrigation and Drainage Engineering 115, 9-20.

Deverel, S. J., and S. K. Gallanthine. 1988. Relation of Salinity and Selenium in Shallow Groundwater to Hydrologic and Geochemical Processes, Western San Joaquin Valley, California. U.S. Geological Survey, Open File Report 88-336.

Deverel, S. J., and S. P. Millard. 1988. Distribution and mobility of selenium and other trace elements in shallow groundwater of the Western San Joaquin Valley, California. Environ. Sci. Technol. 22(6):697-702.

Elrashidi, M. A., D. C. Adriano, and W. L. Lindsay. 1989. Solubility, speciation, and transformation of selenium in soils. Pp. 51-63 in Selenium in Agriculture and the Environment. Special Publ. No. 23. L. W. Jacobs, ed. American Society of Agronomy, Inc., Madison, Wisconsin.

Freeze, R. A., and J. A. Cherry. 1979. Groundwater. Prentice-Hall, Englewood Cliffs, New Jersey.

Fujii, R., S. J. Deverel, and D. B. Hatfield. 1987. Distribution of Selenium in Soils of Agricultural Fields, Western San Joaquin Valley, California. U.S. Geological Survey, Open File Report 87-467.

Jonez, A. R. 1983. Controlling salinity in the Colorado River basin, the arid West. Pp. 337-348 in Salinity in Water Courses and Reservoirs. R. H. French, ed. Butterworth, Boston.

Klasing, S. A., and S. M. Pilch. 1988. Agricultural drainage water contamination in the San Joaquin Valley: A public health perspective for selenium, boron, and molybdenum. San Joaquin Valley Drainage Program, 2800 Cottage Way, Rm. W-2143, Sacramento, California.

Klasing, S. A., and M. B. Schenker. 1988. Public health implications of elevated dietary selenium. In Selenium Contents in Animal and Human Food Crops Grown in California. R. Tanji, ed. Publication 3330. University of California Salinity/Drainage Task Force. Cooperative Extension, University of California, Division of Agriculture and Natural Resources. 102 pp.

Lakin, H. W. 1972. Selenium accumulation in soils and its absorption by plants and animals. In Geochemical Environment in Relation to Health and Disease. H. L. Cannon and H. C. Hopps, eds. Special Paper 140. Geological Society of America, Boulder, Colorado.

Letey, J., C. Roberts, M. Penberth, and C. Vasek. 1986. An Agricultural Dilemma: Drainage Water and Toxics Disposal in the San Joaquin Valley. Special Publication 3319. Agricultural Experiment Station. University of California, Riverside. Division of Agriculture and Natural Resources.

Levander, O. A. 1986. Selenium. Pp. 209-280 in Trace Elements in Human and Animal Nutrition. Vol. 2. 5th Ed. W. Mertz, ed. Academic Press, New York.

Longnecker, M. P. 1989. Selenium: The public health connection. Health and Environment Digest 3(3), 1-3.

National Research Council, Assembly of Life Sciences, Committee on Medical and Biological Effects of Environmental Pollutants. 1976. Selenium. National Academy of Sciences, Washington, D.C.

National Research Council, Food and Nutrition Board, Committee on Dietary Allowances. 1980. Recommended Dietary Allowances, 9th Ed. National Academy Press, Washington, D.C.

Olson, O. E. 1986. Selenium toxicity in animals with an emphasis on man. Journal of the American College of Toxicology 5, 45-70.

Oster, J. D., J. E. Tracy, J. L. Meyer, and M. J. Snyder. 1988. Selenium in or near the southern Coastal Range: well waters and vegetable crops. Pp. 51-55 in Selenium Contents in Animal and Human Food Crops Grown in California. R. Tanji, ed. University of California Salinity/Drainage Task Force. Cooperative Extension, University of California, Division of Agriculture and Natural Resources, Publication 3330. 102 pp.

Public Law 93-320. 1974. United States Statutes at Large, 93rd Congress, 2nd Session, Vol. 88 (Part I): 266-275.

Rosenfeld, I., and O. A. Beath. 1964. Selenium: Geobotany, Biochemistry, and Nutrition. Academic Press, New York.

San Joaquin Valley Drainage Program (SJVDP). 1987. Developing Options: An Overview of Efforts to Solve Agricultural Drainage and Drainage-Related Problems in the San Joaquin Valley. San Joaquin Valley Drainage Program, 2800 Cottage Way, Rm. W-2143, Sacramento, California.

Shacklette, H. T., and J. G. Boerngen. 1984. Elemental concentrations in soils and other surface materials of the conterminous United States. Geological Survey Progress Paper 1272.

Tracy, J. E., J. D. Oster, and R. J. Beaver. 1989. Selenium in a southern Coastal Range of California: Well waters, mapped geologic units and related elements. J. Environ. Qual., in press.

U.S. Committee on Irrigation and Drainage (USCID). 1986. Toxic Substances in Agricultural Water Supply and Drainage: Defining the Problem. Proceedings of 1986 Regional Meetings. U.S. Committee on Irrigation and Drainage, Denver, Colorado.

U.S. Fish and Wildlife Service. 1982a. Regional Resource Plan. Volume II. Central Valley of California Section. U.S. Fish and Wildlife Service, Portland, Oregon. 20 pp.

U.S. Fish and Wildlife Service. 1982b. Regional Resource Plan. Volume IV. Central Valley of California Section. U.S. Fish and Wildlife Service, Portland, Oregon. 15 pp.

U.S. Fish and Wildlife Service. May 1986. North American Waterfowl Management Plan: A Strategy for Cooperation. U.S. Department of the Interior, Washington, D.C.

3
Understanding the Institutional Dimensions of an Environmental Problem

The complexity of the hydrological, geological, chemical, and ecological factors described in Chapter 2 poses a tremendous management challenge, but, in fact, these factors are only part of the picture. They are joined and often exacerbated by an equally complex and conflicting maze of political, social, economic, legal, administrative, and other institutional factors. The technical complexities relate to defining the nature, extent, remediations, and consequences of an environmental problem and the responses proposed. The institutional complexities affect problem awareness and the acceptance and effectiveness of proposed responses. They take on added significance if the level of technical understanding is uncertain.

Typically, it is for institutional (e.g., social and political) reasons that some change in the environment is judged to be a problem rather than merely a change. These same institutional factors will then influence the choice of a response. Because institutional and scientific considerations are entwined, responses must be based on an understanding of the complex interactions that can occur between these two dimensions. The institutional barriers often are more difficult to overcome than the technical problems. In addition, the separation and fragmentation of institutional interests and responsibilities make it hard to develop a coordinated strategy for water use planning.

The term "institutions" is used in many ways and thus can be confusing. At one level, "institutions" is used to mean agencies. However, this definition is too limited. The term "institutions" encompasses much more than the few government bodies with responsibility for resource management

53

and enforcement of relevant laws. The concept also includes administrative organizations, social customs, regulations, policies, and laws. Institutional analysis must consider economic arrangements such as pricing policies and constraints, subsidies, water marketing, water allocation mechanisms, and combining surface and ground water management. It must take into account the potential of different tax schemes (incentives and disincentives), rules, regulations, guidelines, and administrative interpretations, as well as the creation of alternative institutional authorities.

This chapter addresses how institutional factors contribute to the creation and continuation of irrigation-induced water quality problems. It also discusses how these institutional dimensions sometimes impede responses. Although economic issues, social issues, organizational influences, legal issues, and political issues are covered separately, in reality these influences are intricately interrelated.

ECONOMIC FACTORS

Economic factors are a critical institutional issue to be considered when attempting to understand the nature and consequences of irrigation-induced water quality problems. One step in every problem-solving endeavor is to assess the proposed solutions in light of their economic viability (see Chapter 5). However, it is equally important to understand the setting in a broader economic sense—to understand historic economic influences and current economic pressures.

Perhaps the most pervasive economic issue contributing to the creation of irrigation-related water quality problems and affecting the choice and success of solutions is the cost of water. The availability of water of adequate quality, in sufficient amounts, and at an affordable price determines the viability of any effort to settle or to produce crops on arid and semiarid lands. Without water, such land can be almost worthless for farming (at least as measured by the market). With water it is worth thousands of dollars per acre. Building large reservoirs, transporting water long distances, and distributing it over large areas are costly undertakings. Thus the true costs of water supplied by large irrigation projects are generally too high for farmers to pay without subsidies.

One traditional approach used to keep the price of water artificially low has been to exclude the costs of a drainage system when an irrigation project is first planned and built. Because drainage facilities are not needed at the inception of a project, the costs of building them can be delayed in the early phases of project proposal. This has the effect of making the project appear to be much more economical than it would have appeared if drainage costs had not been deferred.

Ignoring the costs of environmental degradation, overestimating crop yields and prices, and underestimating construction and operation costs—whether intentionally or not—also help reduce the apparent cost of irrigation projects. In the West, however, even these strategies were inadequate to overcome the economic realities of irrigated agriculture. Water was still inordinately expensive.

To compensate, other subsidies were adopted. One was to eliminate interest payments in computing the cost of irrigation water. Another was to impose very loose repayment terms—allowing the farmers' financial condition to dictate how much they would actually pay.

The net effect of these subsidies is substantial. Farmers in the North Platte Project in Nebraska and Wyoming annually pay an estimated $0.22/acre/yr for water that would carry an unsubsidized price of $8.18 (U.S. Department of the Interior, 1988). Irrigators in the Bonneville Unit of the Central Utah Project contribute $17.84/acre/yr toward repayment; the federal government's share is $306.40. And the amount of subsidies is increasing with newer projects: irrigation waters from the Animas-LaPlata Project in southwestern Colorado will sell for $40.60/acre/yr although the real cost is estimated at $673.47. Farmers in the Central Arizona Project will pay $213.40/acre/yr for water that costs an estimated $542/acre/yr (U.S. Department of the Interior, 1988). (Table 3.1 provides other examples, although it should be noted that these figures are not directly comparable because they are calculated on a rate-per-acre-foot basis.)

Figures were compiled by the U.S. Bureau of Reclamation (USBR) at the request of Congress in 1988 to illustrate the range of the real costs of water in the West. (All such estimates should be approached cautiously because they can vary significantly depending on how interest is incorporated. This can greatly change the degree, but not the direction, of the subsidy.) According to these estimates, in 1986 western farmers received an irrigation subsidy of about $534 million from the federal government, for an average of $54/acre of irrigated land. The total annual subsidy of California's Central Valley Project in 1986 was $135.4 million, about one-fourth of the national total. The total value of the irrigation subsidy from 1902 through 1986 is roughly estimated to have been $9.8 billion (U.S. Department of the Interior, 1988).

Nationally over the past 10 years, an average of 38 percent of that subsidized water was used to grow crops that the government considered surplus, including cotton, rice, wheat, corn, oats, barley, sorghum, and soybeans. In 1986 alone, farmers using USBR water to irrigate surplus crops received about $203 million in irrigation subsidies (U.S. Department of the Interior, 1988). This "double subsidy"—obtained when some producers participate in commodity subsidy programs and receive subsidized irrigation water—is of particular concern (Moore and McGuckin, 1988).

These subsidy policies contribute to three effects. First, they ensure

TABLE 3.1 Subsidized and Full Cost Prices per Acre-Foot of Water for 18 Reclamation Districts

District	Subsidized Rate ($)	"Full Cost" Rate ($)
Black Canyon, ID	1.41	15.77
Coachella, CA	7.00	26.27
Columbia Basin East, WA	4.19	41.16
Elephant Butte, NM	6.45	24.43
Farwell, NE	10.50	135.50
Glenn-Colusa, CA	1.46	17.85
Goleta, CA	59.24	263.12
Goshen, WY	4.22	22.96
Grand Valley, CO	1.18	31.10
Imperial, CA	4.75	11.00
Lower Yellowstone, MT	5.28	34.62
Lugert-Altus, OK	18.58	143.19
Milk River, MT	7.79	119.13
Moon Lake, UT	1.75	7.04
Oroville-Tonasket, WA	11.47	21.33
Truckee-Carson, NV	2.19	33.46
Wellton Mohawk, AZ	4.80	29.58
Westlands, CA	15.80	67.56

NOTE: Subsidized rates and full cost rates were calculated according to section 203(a) of the Reclamation Reform Act of 1982. These calculations do not include opportunity costs and thus are conservative.

SOURCE: U.S. Department of the Interior, 1980.

that the projects are rarely paid for by farmers, because the USBR sets annual charges too low to recover the capital costs. In a given year it often costs more just to operate most systems than the farmers pay for the water.

Second, they create an economy based on subsidized water, one that may lack the financial resources and incentives to deal with the inevitable problems that irrigated agriculture creates. The West has many marginal irrigation projects supporting farmers whose economic existence is dependent on water subsidies. Over time the dependency becomes fundamental to local lifestyles, and there is an expectation of unending support. Such expectations are capitalized in land values, and any change in the status quo will inflict large costs on the farming community.

Third, they reduce the incentives that encourage farmers to use water efficiently. The economic and legal factors determining water use in the West have created an immense irony. Water is in many ways the most valuable commodity in the arid West and the basis of much of its wealth. Yet because it is sold at artificially low prices, farmers often treat water as if it were a free commodity. Crops are overirrigated because that is easier than managing the water carefully, and canals leak because it is not economical to line or fix them.

Thus, the subsidization of irrigation water appears to be a major culprit contributing to irrigation-induced water quality problems. The low cost of water results in more water being used, it encourages farmers to cultivate less desirable lands, and it leads to increased leaching from subsurface flow. Current water use patterns also diminish the amount of fresh water left in streams to dilute contaminants and carry them out to sea, and they have stimulated the drainage of wetlands, with a concomitant loss of their ecological functions and diversity. Water subsidies do bring well-known benefits, particularly in the social realm, but it is increasingly important to recognize the full scope of disadvantages as well.

A final economic reality that should be mentioned is the problem of tight budgets. Federal, state, and local governments all are facing serious financial constraints. Proposals to undertake expensive activities to build new water development projects or to correct problems caused by existing projects receive greater scrutiny now than in the past.

The difficult and important question of who will pay for whatever actions are adopted also arises. Will it be the farmers, many of whom have limited capability to pay for major new undertakings? Should they pay, for instance, for new wildlife habitats or in-stream flows? Or will some (or perhaps all) of the costs be underwritten by the state's and/or the nation's taxpayers? It is not likely or reasonable that these regional costs be assumed totally on a national scale. Technical solutions for irrigation-induced problems may exist, but it will prove difficult to resolve who is to pay for those solutions.

SOCIAL FACTORS

Social acceptability has proved to be an increasingly visible criterion for addressing environmental concerns such as irrigation-induced water quality problems. It is particularly important to recognize the fundamental role that social issues play in setting the stage for both the creation of irrigation-related problems and the choice of solutions.

The United States has used laws, policies, and economics to establish an agricultural society in the West that depends on subsidized water. Any change in rights will change the distribution of income, and the people who have benefited from the original system will resist any attempts to change it. This social dimension is well reflected by the political powers it creates and the agencies that serve it. Together these forces create the laws and regulations that preserve, reinforce, and expand the reliance on economic subsidies.

The U.S. Bureau of Reclamation system was originally established with the intention of promoting the small family farm. The Reclamation Act of 1902 originally limited the water available so that no farm could receive water for more than 160 acres. This figure was revised to 320 acres, 160 acres each for husband and wife. The intent was to promote an equitable distribution of social and economic benefits, but this limitation was never rigorously enforced. More often than not, reclamation projects and the economics of scale led to large farm holdings, and the wealth created was concentrated in a small percentage of the population (Goodall and Sullivan, 1985).

As agricultural practices changed, many irrigators avoided the 160-acre limit through complicated trusts and rental agreements, and by registering land in the names of different family members. Because of the complicated mechanisms used to avoid the limit in many areas, it is difficult to say with certainty what the average farm size is in many reclamation projects. But the concept that the benefits of subsidized water are accruing largely to small family farms is a myth. In California, for instance, corporate farms owned by firms such as Southern Pacific, Chevron USA, Getty Oil, Shell Oil, and Prudential Insurance are estimated to use more than two-thirds of the state's agricultural water (Martin, 1989).

The net effect of this situation is that, politically and socially, the reclamation system has created many farms throughout the West that probably could not survive without the substantial subsidies they receive. This cadre of farmers adds to the political pressures that resist changing the existing system. And they have limited capacity to take on additional financial burdens required to correct irrigation-induced water quality problems. At the same time, a large portion of the subsidies goes not to small farmers but to larger enterprises that probably could afford to pay more realistic prices for their water supplies as well as the costs associated with water quality improvement.

This subsidy system does not exist in a vacuum. The subsidies have to be paid by someone. Some are financed from within the region; for instance, municipalities and industries pay higher rates and end up supporting the costs of new state or regional water projects so that farmers can continue to receive low-cost supplies. The state taxpayer picks up other expenses. Taxpayers outside the region also pay many of the subsidies. As the nation adds other subsidies—principally in the form of commodity price supports—the problems are exacerbated and become even more difficult to solve. The dilemma created is that short-term benefits accrue primarily to the agricultural sector (and perhaps to the public in the form of lower food costs, although this has not been clearly demonstrated), while in the long run the costs with respect to tax outlays and environmental degradation are borne by those who may not have experienced the benefits.

High subsidy levels increasingly are being questioned. It is not only the subsidies that people are questioning, but also the very use that is being made of the water. For the population served by public supplies, the average domestic per capita water use in western states is 143 gallons per person per day, compared to 105 gallons in the rest of the country (Solley et al., 1988). Many of the West's new residents have brought with them not only additional demands for the region's limited water supplies, but also different perceptions about how the water can be used most beneficially and treasured as a valuable commodity. Historically, most of the West's water has gone to rural economic uses such as farming, ranching, and mining. But the West—long romanticized for its rural frontiers—is becoming increasingly urban, and these urban residents often have different ideas about water use. Nationally, 73.7 percent of the population lives in urban areas, but in California the percentage is 91.3 and in Arizona, 83.8 (Statistical Abstract, 1988).

Urban residents bring different values and priorities. They may be more interested in using water to sustain their urban jobs, water their lawns, and provide recreational opportunities than to irrigate crops (El-Ashry and Gibbons, 1986). And to the extent that the existing water allocation system allows water markets to determine how the water is used, these urban users can often pay much more than rural users pay. Industries and municipalities have indicated a willingness to pay hundreds and, in some cases, thousands of dollars for water that costs farmers tens of dollars. On a smaller scale, the increasing wealth of some segments of society creates an increased demand for recreation, including wildlife habitats, wild rivers, and streams for fishing.

The shift from a rural to an increasingly urban population is not the only reason for the change in values that is occurring. There is a greater recognition now of the costs to society in terms of ecological change. Diminishing wildlife and waterfowl populations, the extinction of plant and animal species, and the ever-shrinking availability of clean water supplies are viewed as indicators of undesirable ecological changes. Many citizens now place more emphasis on environmental protection, clean up, and enhancement. For example, leaving water in the stream was once considered tantamount to wasting it; most states did not consider in-stream flow to be a beneficial water use. That is no longer the case. Keeping water in the stream is seen as having a high value by many westerners, and all western states now recognize some form of in-stream flow rights.

The increased growth in population and economic activity has affected not only the quantity of water in the region's rivers but the quality of that water as well. As the West has grown, so have waste-producing human activities. The expansion of cropland and livestock operations, the growth in industrial output, the increased amount of land cleared for residential

Society's values have changed with time, and many citizens now place more emphasis on environmental protection. Although irrigation remains the largest water user in the West, there is an increased demand for water for other, less tangible uses such as wildlife habitat, wild rivers, and recreation.
CREDIT: Soil Conservation Service, D. Schuhart.

and commercial purposes—indeed almost all the activities associated with this growth—increase the amount of pollutants entering streams and rivers. Society traditionally has used rivers and streams as pipelines to carry its wastes, but this approach is increasingly inadequate as the amount of water in the rivers and streams diminishes or where the waterways are rendered unfit for human and other uses by uncontrolled pollution or incomplete treatment.

Arid regions face an inherent dilemma—development consumes the water needed to carry away resulting wastes, at the same time increasing the amount of wastes it produces. Some of this pollution can be controlled, but much cannot. The increasing loads of pollution will inevitably hasten the deterioration of the region's scarce water resources.

The changing demographics, increasing income, and shift in values that have caused these changes are likely to continue. And the resulting changes in priorities, combined with a relatively inflexible water allocation system and continually diminishing supplies of available water, will generate increasing conflicts. There is no additional water, just more demand on the limited supplies available.

AGENCIES AND ORGANIZATIONS

Another critical area to be considered in any problem-solving endeavor is the influence of agencies and organizations, including both governmental and nongovernmental bodies.

Organizational influences change over time to reflect the nation's changes in priorities and values. Two decades ago, the USBR was the primary federal agency concerned with irrigated agriculture, and it was primarily concerned with only one objective: assuring an abundant supply of inexpensive water for farmers. Questions of environmental degradation and the values of wildlife and in-stream flows generally were rarely considered because society did not give these issues the high priority it does today.

Since then, however, agencies such as the U.S. Environmental Protection Agency have been created, and others like the U.S. Fish and Wildlife Service (USFWS) have become much more involved in the health of the environment on which wildlife depend. Similar changes have taken place at the state and local level, and in most cases, this proliferation of regulatory and management agencies has been matched by a proliferation of relevant laws (Box 3.A), regulations, treaties, and court decisions.

A similar proliferation of organizations has taken place in the non-governmental sector. Numerous public groups interested in some part of the problem have come into existence, and their membership has grown rapidly. Small and large associations also exist at the producer and business level to attempt to protect their interests.

Many examples of overlapping agency jurisdictions exist, as do examples of areas where there are significant gaps in responsibilities. Water delivery organizations are often separate from water drainage organizations. The upper and lower reaches of the same stream may be the responsibility of different institutions. There may be a dozen or more irrigation districts within one county. Agencies and regulators concerned about public health differ from those responsible for wildlife or water quality. Political and agency boundaries often cross hydrological boundaries, making the coordinated planning of water resources difficult. Most often, the agencies responsible for the activities that caused a problem have no responsibilities, or incentives, for considering or solving the dilemmas they have helped create. In fact, it may be in the agency's best interest, or that of its clients, to deny that the problem exists. Again, the result is often a conflict between agencies with different mandates.

BOX 3.A   Some Important Laws and Statutes Relevant to Activities in California's San Joaquin Valley

Federal Statutes:

Migratory Bird Treaty Act. This act prohibits the unlawful taking or possession of any migratory bird in accordance with treaties signed by the United States and the USSR (1976), Japan (1972), Mexico (1936), and Great Britain (1916). "Taking" is defined as the act or attempt to "pursue, hunt, shoot, capture, collect, or kill . . ." (16 USC Section 715n). Exceptions require a permit from the secretary of the interior. This act traditionally has been viewed as a hunting violations law, but recent cases have used a broader interpretation of unintentional nonhunting takings. The USFWS has primary responsibility for enforcing this statute.

Endangered Species Act. This act is an attempt to address the global problem of the increasing number of species faced with extinction. It requires all U.S. agency actions to be carried out in a manner that will not jeopardize the continued existence of an endangered species. It also requires the secretary of the interior to consult with other federal agencies with jurisdiction over an endangered species. In recent years, the process for listing critical habitats for endangered species has become more complex.

Federal Water Pollution Control Act. This 1972 legislation attempts to ensure clean water (the "swimmable, fishable" goal) for the nation. The Clean Water Act (CWA) of 1977 is a revision of this legislation. The act greatly broadened the role of the Environmental Protection Agency by directing it to set effluent standards and regulate the amount of a pollutant that can be discharged based on its environmental effects. Although the CWA is the strongest federal water pollution control act on record, it is not directly applicable to the situation in the San Joaquin Valley because irrigation return flows from agriculture are classified as nonpoint pollution, which was consciously excluded from the act. However, this does not prevent individual states from instituting stricter agricultural effluent standards. The Environmental Protection Agency has primary responsibility for this statute.

California Statutes:

Porter-Cologne Water Quality Control Act. This major legislation, effective since 1970, lays out California's enforcement and remedies for state water law. Its goal is to protect the health, safety, and welfare of state residents and to protect water quality for the use and enjoyment of the state's people. The act established the State Water Resources Control Board and nine regional boards that are responsible for achieving these goals. It granted them broad authority to regulate hazardous waste discharges and to formulate and implement water quality control plans. These plans must consider a variety of beneficial uses of water, regional economic factors, and environmental characteristics. Regional boards are empowered to confer

Continued

BOX 3.A Continued

civil fines, restraining orders, or injunctions to regulate any party discharging waste to state waters without the proper permit.

Toxic Pits Cleanup Act. This act became effective in 1984 in response to the growing problem of water pollution caused by discharges of hazardous waste on land. Hazardous waste is designated by "its toxicity, mobility, or presence in a land disposal environment, or its ability to accumulate in plants or animals" (California Health and Safety Code, 25208(b)). The act prohibits discharge of any liquid hazardous waste into a surface impoundment after January 1, 1989, unless specific equipment is installed and the site is monitored carefully. Hazardous discharges are prohibited to surface impoundments after June 30, 1988, if the impoundment is within one-half mile upgradient from a potential drinking water source. Regional water quality control boards inspect all surface impoundments at least once a year and dischargers failing to meet requirements are fined.

The Safe Drinking Water and Toxic Enforcement Act. This 1986 act, known as Proposition 65, is perhaps the strictest regulation of toxic substances in drinking water in the nation. It requires all consumer products containing chemicals known to cause cancer or reproductive harm to carry warnings, and prohibits businesses from knowingly discharging listed chemicals into drinking water sources. The governor is required to update and publish annually a list of chemicals known to cause cancer or reproductive toxicity; among the substances on the list are benzene, lead, vinyl chloride, chromium, arsenic, asbestos, DDT, and PCBs. Other substances are expected to be added in the future. The act also provides penalties for violators, with the goal of shifting the cost of hazardous waste cleanup from the taxpayer to the offending parties. This act, however, only applies to businesses with more than 10 employees, and public agencies such as irrigation districts, state and federal agencies, municipalities, and the military are exempt. Hence it does not apply to most irrigation-related water quality problems. A proposal to extend the law to cover public agencies has been proposed.

SOURCE: After Letey et al., 1986.

As an example, the 1982 discovery of high selenium levels and deformed waterfowl at Kesterson National Wildlife Refuge (NWR) focused attention on the conflicts in the missions of two federal agencies, both within the U.S. Department of the Interior. The USBR operates from a long-standing congressional mandate to promote settlement in the West by providing water for agriculture. The USFWS has many responsibilities, including the protection and maintenance of migratory bird populations. But the Kesterson issue transcended the interests of these agencies, forcing them into an uneasy partnership.

This complex organizational backdrop reflects an equally complex legal structure affecting the use of water in western states. Over the years, western states have developed a body of water law that in many

The structures and functions of the nation's resource management agencies have changed over time to reflect changes in priorities and values. Agencies with sometimes conflicting missions, such as the U.S. Bureau of Reclamation and the U.S. Fish and Wildlife Service, are facing increased pressure to work cooperatively to ensure that the varied needs of society are balanced. Here, a refuge manager at the Deer Flat National Wildlife Refuge, located within the bureau's Boise Project, monitors geese nesting on the Snake River. CREDIT: U.S. Bureau of Reclamation, J. D. Roderick.

ways contributes to the types of problems discovered at Kesterson NWR and elsewhere. For instance, the legal system of water rights and water allocation in western states discourages water conservation, because the person saving it often is not allowed, for a complicated set of reasons, to sell any water that is saved. Thus farmers often perceive that conserving water will result in their losing the right to it, and they perceive an incentive to use as much as possible to establish a right to a larger amount.

Another dilemma that involves both organizational and legal influences relates to the allocation of water. In many basins, the legal system has already allocated more water than is available in most years. For instance, the courts have allocated 15 million acre-feet of water from the Colorado River annually to the seven basin states, and by treaty Mexico is entitled to 1.5 million acre-feet. Despite these legal demands for 16.5 million acre-feet, the river's average flow is about 14 million acre-feet (Weatherford and Jacoby, 1975). It is becoming increasingly clear that legislatures may provide exemptions from the laws of man, but not from the laws of nature.

LEGAL ISSUES

The overall legal and regulatory milieu shapes both the causes of irrigation-related problems and the acceptability of solutions. It is not entirely possible to separate legal issues from other institutional issues because laws define the operating parameters of government agencies, regulate the use and transferability of water resources, and are intertwined with many other fundamental institutional issues. These issues range from rights of appropriators to water under the prior appropriation doctrine to contract rights of parties who have contracted to receive water from an irrigation district, and from rights of irrigation districts under contracts with the USBR to rights of members of the public under the public trust doctrine.

The legal issues involved in solving irrigation-induced water quality problems are complex, and they are closely tied to the organization issues (Table 3.2). All organizations are governed by sets of legal rules that confer authority to act and that may give them standing to intervene in the formulation and enforcement of any solutions aimed at addressing irrigation-related issues.

One often-discussed response to the San Joaquin Valley's problem is reducing the consumptive use of water by particular irrigators. The "reasonable use" doctrine of California provides one possible vehicle for reducing water use by irrigators. The reasonable use doctrine suggests that an irrigator can only use as much water as is "reasonably" necessary to grow his crops. One unanswered question, however, is whether this device has the breadth to reach and regulate the quality of water discharged by individual irrigators. Other questions that would need to be considered are whether individuals downstream would have standing to raise the issue, whether the California Department of Water Resources could enforce the doctrine, and whether the Water Resources Control Board could enforce it by making existing permits contingent on reduced discharge. Another legal issue would be whether this approach would constitute an unconstitutional taking of property if the permit conditions in effect put farmers out of business or measurably decreased their profit.

One legal obstacle to drainage reduction based on legislation that imposes across-the-board reductions is that it may have greatly disparate

TABLE 3.2 Agencies Active in the San Joaquin Valley Example and Their General Legal Foundations

Agency*	General Legal Responsibilities
U.S. Bureau of Reclamation	Federal reclamation law
California Department of Water Resources	California water law
Irrigation and drainage districts in the Central Valley	State and local laws and regulations controlling the operations of irrigation districts
State of California Water Resources Control Board	State water quality laws
Department of Health Services	State public health laws
U.S. Environmental Protection Agency	Federal environmental laws, Safe Drinking Water Act, Clean Water Act, National Environmental Policy Act
Resource management agencies such as the Wildlife Service and the California Department of Fish and Game	State wildlife protection laws, Endangered Species Act, and Migratory Bird Treaty Act

*The allocation of responsibilities for enforcement of these various laws is extremely complex. The water quality and quantity and public health laws in general are enforced by the State of California through its administrative agencies. The reclamation law is enforced by the United States or the irrigation districts depending on which party is seeking relief.

impacts, giving rise to claims of denial of equal protection under the law. Existing contracts may allocate quantities of water equally among irrigators, but the exact quantum of noxious drainage per user is very difficult to determine. This raises complex legal issues such as who should bear the burden of proof as to individual impact on the system, the degree of the burden of proof required, and the power of the legislature to penalize some for the pollution of others.

Another legal issue raised by existing water law doctrine is that the prevailing state law concept of "beneficial use" may work directly against programs attempting to encourage a reduction in water use. Under state law, beneficial use is the measure and limit of water rights. Those who voluntarily reduce their water consumption may be reducing the size of their contractual or property right in the water.

Another basic legal issue is whether to encourage the adoption of stringent water quality standards at the downstream end of a drainage system and simply allow these standards to dictate all conservation behavior upstream. For instance, in the San Joaquin Valley, water quality standards for selenium, boron, and salinity downstream of the districts could be determined in a public forum by state and regional boards, and these standards could in effect set the farmers' use of irrigation water. If across-the-board regulations are adopted regarding quality, the application of those standards is likely to be challenged in court.

Another complicating factor is that agricultural return flows do not typically fall under regulations dealing with point source pollution. In the long term, however, the irony may be that as a result of not being subject to the regulations, agricultural interests are ineligible for federal grants under the Clean Water Act, should such grants become available.

An alternative to the adoption of broad regulatory standards or attempted enforcement of broad water law doctrines such as reasonable use would be to provide economic incentives to irrigators to use less water. However, federal, state, and local laws may contain provisions that affect this solution. First, internal district allocation rules may provide a deterrent to water conservation because water is generally contracted on a district-wide basis, and individual farmers who cut back on consumption will simply see the water made available to other users in the district without receiving any compensation for their conservation. Furthermore, the USBR policy of not allowing carry-over storage from year to year would deter conservation because the water saved would be lost if not used within the irrigation season. Finally, there is the very difficult question of who actually owns the water to be sold. Is it the federal government, the district, or the farmer? Added to this, of course, is the role of the "public trust" doctrine, wherein the public at large may hold an interest, as yet not fully specified, in some quantity of water for public purposes. The answer is probably that ownership is a partnership.

Constraints on water transfers also exist in federal reclamation law. However, the degree of enforcement of those constraints often changes with changes in the administration in Washington, D.C. During the years of the Carter administration, for instance, USBR policy suggested that the title to water rights under federal projects, if not fully vested in the federal government, certainly bore the burden of a federal trust that limited usage to irrigation; in particular, it suggested that the use must be on appurtenant lands. More recently the view has changed to suggest more flexibility in usage. Unfortunately for the proponents of free transfers, the right to use of the water is based on long-term contracts, which are made not with individual farmers but with water districts. Such contracts would need to be reevaluated and renegotiated if individual farmers were to be given full economic incentives to transfer their water rights.

In addition, state law vests substantial regulatory control in state regulatory agencies. No water transfer can be completed unless it can be demonstrated that it does not injure other water rights holders. Thus, although the water contracts are between a federal agency and a private individual, movement of water and shifts from ground to surface water may affect other rights holders, and the state therefore becomes involved. Also, this restriction against causing injury is being reinterpreted as applying to the community as a whole. Regional economic and social effects will have to be considered before some transfers will be allowed.

Within a district the issue is somewhat complicated by the contractual nature of farmers' rights and the internal rules for water allocation. Nevertheless, the issue of impairment of other water rights inevitably arises when major water rights transfers are sought. In addition to protecting the other water users, the agency before whom a transfer is sought must evaluate the potential injury to wildlife and other entities reflecting the public trust interests inherent in water usage in California. At first glance, it would seem that the public trust would be overwhelmingly served by reducing water consumption. It is unclear, however, whether the decrease of the public trust values in one area can be balanced against benefits such as a reduction in trace element contamination. Furthermore, any transfers that reduced wetlands would have to include mitigation by creating new wetlands elsewhere. These mitigation efforts could certainly be a cost to the potential transfer.

From both a legal and economic standpoint, new legal developments in California that purport to make certain water conveyance systems more akin to common carriers and to allow water consumers to use unused conveyance space are encouraging. However, it remains to be seen whether there is sufficient space for conveying transferred water. Likewise, it remains to be seen how reclamation law would permit the conveyed water to be priced. If it were made available to farmers at irrigation prices and if the farmers, after taking delivery, were to make the water available to municipal or industrial users, contracts would likely have to be written that clearly stated who was to receive the profit—the USBR, the water district, or individual farmers. If the transfer were to be considered to create a supplemental benefit for the district, provisions of the Reclamation Reform Act of 1982 might come into play and lead to legal entanglements. If the government were no worse off, and the transfer were from one existing contractor to another, the transition might be exempt under existing USBR regulations.

To attempt a transfer and to run the gauntlet of the various federal and state laws and regulations require money for attorneys' fees and experts. As experience is gained, the process of negotiating each transfer will become cheaper, but the overall costs may still be quite high. Whether the benefits of a sale of a portion of one's water to a potential customer will justify the expense to the average farmer is not clear, nor is it clear whether smaller districts will make such an effort based on economic incentives alone.

There is also a vague requirement in both federal law and in federal water contracts that defines the permissible regional limits on the use of water. To the degree that these requirements are imbedded in congressional acts, it will take an act of Congress to change them. If they are set forward in existing federal contracts, then they can be changed at the agency level.

Changing a federal contract creates no serious legal concerns when the act of the federal agency is essentially nondiscretionary or makes no basic change in a federal project. However, a federal employee's decision to exercise discretion to permit major water transfers from one location to another would likely trigger the operation of the National Environmental Policy Act and would require the preparation either of a document finding no significant impact or, in some cases, of a full environmental impact statement.

The development of an environmental impact statement would undoubtedly lead to the realization that transferring major quantities of water out of one basin and into another, or even simply changing the use of water within a basin, could have substantial impacts on endangered species and many forms of wildlife, particularly waterfowl.

There are also practical legal problems associated with the task of transferring water rights. One problem might arise from the lack of technically competent people available to address the legal issues involved. A case that involves a transfer of any large quantity of water from one location to another also presents immense burden-of-proof issues. The burden of proof will no doubt be on the person seeking the transfer, who will face two tasks. The first is to convince the federal government, the state, the irrigation district, and fellow farmers that he or she has the legal right to sell the water. Although formidable, this is mainly a legal issue. The second, more difficult task is to prove that the actions are consistent with the public interest. What constitutes the public interest is a question of incredibly complex dimensions. No doubt, there is public interest in seeing water moved to higher-value uses, but there is also public interest in promoting rural, cultural, and environmental values.

Proving that the transfer is consistent with the public interest is a substantial task if the farmer intends to decrease his surface use and increase ground water pumping. It can involve extensive use of computer models to demonstrate that the cone of depression caused by the increased use will not create problems for other wells and will not interfere with surface water drains. In addition, even if the impairment issues are resolved, there is still the issue of whether the transfer will provide benefits by reducing pollution. In many cases it will be extraordinarily difficult to show that the source of the pollution will even be affected by an individual transfer, much less abated in some way.

Finally, the cadre of participants in a water transfer will be extensive. Many special interest groups will intervene to show that their proposals will be more beneficial to the public interest than the transfer will be. Persons seeking tougher downstream water quality standards may feel threatened by what they perceive as a temporary solution when what is needed to support the public interest is more rigorous river protection standards.

Water quality and water quantity issues have been treated separately throughout U.S. history. California is no exception to this rule. This is perhaps best manifested in the fact that federal water allocation contracts have been found to be nondiscretionary exceptions to the National Environmental Policy Act (see discussion above) and note the fact that California has two distinct agencies that address these issues (see Table 3.2). Hearings are currently pending on the relevant stream systems, and their outcome may well have a great deal of impact.

Even though this section has emphasized obstacles to drainage water cleanup, there are various positive signals as well. The USBR is facing a changing mission as the need for new construction diminishes and the need for more efficient management emerges. They have taken a position in favor of water marketing that bodes well for that possibility should other problems be resolved. In addition, California law has moved in the direction of allowing economic incentives for conservation practices.

Finally, institutional analysis should not totally reject the possibility of "top-down standardization." In response to excessive salinity pollution in Mexico, the Colorado River basin states have been very effective in setting salinity standards for the Colorado River and, with the help of federal money, reducing salinity levels at the border between Mexico and the United States. This concept of treating drainage from a federal irrigation project as a shared federal and state responsibility may well be a model that could operate in this arena.

POLITICAL FACTORS

Finally, irrigation-related problems and any proposed solutions must be evaluated in terms of political realities. Although this is a difficult task because the political process is rarely clear-cut, it is essential to the process of choosing appropriate solutions. In the West, after all, water is a political issue that generates unusual passion.

The political setting has played perhaps the most critical role in creating situations conducive to irrigation-related problems. The decision to irrigate the West was first and foremost a political one: policymakers decided to promote the settlement of the West and "make the deserts bloom." It was a political decision clearly designed to promote social goals, and it was translated into law via the Reclamation Act of 1902. It occurred at a time when there was great belief in the ability of technology and engineering to overcome almost any obstacle that nature might put in the way. It created in the West a social and economic system that cannot survive without substantial support, and it is politics that provide that support. In short, the political system created many of the problems now being faced, it created a structure that prevented them from being addressed effectively early on, and it will ultimately determine what solutions will be implemented (Worster, 1985).

The importance of political influences—both past and present—is illustrated clearly in the San Joaquin Valley. There, as elsewhere in the West, agriculture flourished because political forces exerted pressure in favor of subsidized irrigation development. This, in turn, produced abundant crops, created jobs, and fostered a strong agriculturally based economy. In turn, these benefits built an even stronger political base of support. The region's political, economic, and social ties to irrigated agriculture give its people a great stake in ongoing discussions about how to solve the problems caused by the accumulation of salts and harmful trace elements. For example, agricultural interests were reluctant to have the San Joaquin Valley Drainage Program (SJVDP) discuss any options perceived to be against agriculture, such as the issue of retiring particularly problematic lands from farming. Political influences from another sphere—environmental interests in the San Francisco Bay area—are similarly evident; this view surfaces most visibly in the pressures that prevented the SJVDP from seriously considering ocean disposal as a possible alternative even though many scientists argue that this is a credible option.

Thus political, social, economic, institutional, and legal factors have all contributed substantially to the irrigation-induced water quality problems identified in the San Joaquin Valley and elsewhere in the West. These factors will strongly influence the choice of potential solutions. In many ways, the solutions to the problems the nation faces are hindered less by technical or scientific uncertainties than by social, economic, and legal confrontations. Thus, unless political, economic, social, and institutional means can be brought to bear on the process, it will prove impossible to solve irrigation-induced water quality problems.

CONCLUSIONS

Many factors affect society's ability to respond to irrigation-induced water quality problems. Often, institutional and scientific considerations are entwined, and effective programs to solve such problems require an understanding of the complex interactions that occur between social and physical components. The physical changes and the environmental and social impacts associated with irrigation and its return flow in arid and semiarid regions can be exacerbated or ameliorated by the institutional setting—which involves a maze of sometimes competing interest groups, agencies, laws, and mandates. It is a setting shaped by underlying societal values. However, this institutional separation and fragmentation of interests and responsibilities have made it difficult to develop a coordinated strategy for water resources planning.

Can irrigated agriculture be sustained indefinitely or is it always doomed to fail because of salinization or related problems? Certainly there are abundant examples of failure throughout history. The key to making sustainable production physically possible is maintaining a high level of management and investment to remove and dispose of accumulating salts. The critical difference is the perspective of the time scale involved. As long as the goals are short term and water management is the primary concern, irrigation is doomed to fail. However, if the planning is truly long term and includes a focus on the management of dissolved chemicals, and if it is judged to be in the national interest to pay both the economic and environmental costs, then it should be possible to create a sustainable irrigated agriculture. The critical issue of time frame may be reflected in the choice of technology used to combat irrigation-induced water quality problems, but the underlying decision on strategy is set by political, economic, and social influences.

Solutions to satisfy all the parties affected by irrigation-induced water quality problems will not be easy to find. Difficult trade-offs and compromises will have to be made. The protection of water and land resources provides the foundation for future growth and development. Agriculture is only one of many interests that need a dependable supply of unpolluted water. As populations grow and patterns of water use change, institutions will need to respond. The issue of irrigation drainage water is important, but it is only part of a broader issue: that of managing water resources for the long-term public good. Water quantity and water quality can no longer be addressed separately.

REFERENCES

El-Ashry, M. T., and D. C. Gibbons. 1986. Troubled Waters: New Policies for Managing Water in the American West. Study 6. World Resources Institute, Washington, D.C. October.

Goodall, M. R., and J. D. Sullivan. 1985. Water system entities in California: social and environmental effects. Pp. 71-102 in Special Water Districts: Challenge for the Future. J. N. Carbridge, Jr., ed. Natural Resources Law Center, University of Colorado, Boulder.

Letey, J., C. Roberts, M. Penberth, and C. Vasek. 1986. An Agricultural Dilemma: Drainage Water and Toxics Disposal in the San Joaquin Valley. Special Publication 3319. Agricultural Experiment Station. University of California, Riverside. Division of Agriculture and Natural Resources.

Martin, G. 1989. At the public water trough, The World, San Francisco Sunday Examiner and Chronicle, January 29, p. 12.

Moore, M. R., and C. A. McGuckin. 1988. Program Crop Production and Federal Irrigation Water. Reprinted from Agricultural Resources: Cropland, Water, and Conservation Situation and Outlook Report. AR-12. U.S. Department of Agriculture, Economic Research Service, Washington, D.C.

Solley, W. B., C. F. Merk, and R. R. Pierce. 1988. Estimated use of water in the United States in 1985. Circular 1004. U.S. Geological Survey, Reston, Virginia.

Statistical Abstract. 1988. U.S. Government Printing Office, Washington, D.C.

U.S. Department of the Interior. 1980. Draft Environmental Impact Statement (DEIS), Acreage Limitation, Westwide Report Appendix G (Full Cost Pricing Option), Table 2.

U.S. Department of the Interior. 1988. H.R. 1443. Irrigation Subsidy Legislation: Questions from the Subcommittee on Water and Power Resources of the Committee on Interior and Insular Affairs.

Weatherford, G. D., and G. C. Jacoby. 1975. Impact of energy development on the law of the Colorado River. Natural Resources Journal 15(1), 171-213.

Worster, D. 1985. Rivers of Empire: Water, Aridity, and the Growth of the American West. Pantheon Books, New York.

4
Resolving Problems:
Essential Study Elements

Science serves a critical role in seeking solutions to significant environmental quality problems and mediating the conflicts that arise among parties with different perceptions of a problem and its potential solutions. The San Joaquin Valley Drainage Program (SJVDP) is a clear example of science in this role. Whether in the San Joaquin Valley or elsewhere, science performs key functions in a process that involves collecting and analyzing data, proposing alternative solutions, and articulating trade-offs.

Science deals well with defining the objective properties of water, but it is less able to address issues that involve value judgments. The degree of excellence, or quality, of water is a concept that requires value judgments. This interface between science and human values challenges even the best problem-solving techniques.

In the Kesterson case, for example, science can determine the concentrations of selenium that are toxic to waterfowl or define the relationship between increasing salt concentrations and crop production. But science cannot judge which is more valuable, the crop or the waterfowl, nor can science assign values to predicted outcomes. As was discussed in Chapter 3, it is in this sense that the parallel involvement of ethics, law, economics, politics, and public policy has made the problems in the San Joaquin Valley particularly difficult to define and solve.

Finding solutions to environmental problems like those caused by irrigation drainage requires difficult choices. Thus the equity and effectiveness of the process used to seek, evaluate, and implement potential solutions become critically important. For this reason, good study design is essential.

Concurring with an earlier National Research Council Study, *Ecological Knowledge and Environmental Problem-Solving: Concepts and Case Studies* (National Research Council, 1986), the framework presented here is "in essence, an admonition to think before acting and to use established scientific principles." Although that National Research Council study focused on the environmental impact assessment process, this committee's activities have strongly reinforced many of the same messages. This report also reinforces many points about sound study design for long-term monitoring as were highlighted in another National Research Council study, *River and Dam Management: A Review of the Bureau of Reclamation's Glen Canyon Environmental Studies* (National Research Council, 1987).

The purpose of this chapter is to highlight key elements that the committee believes are essential in addressing complex problems and that are likely to prove important to future research efforts. The chapter introduces five basic functions that characterize problem solving. The first three elements (i.e., recognizing the problem, defining the problem, and collecting and compiling data) are examined at length in this chapter. Chapter 5 examines the final two interpretive elements (identifying and evaluating alternative responses).

This chapter reflects the committee's deliberations and evaluation of the problem-solving process, but it has also benefited from the work of several authors who have explored complex problem solving in depth (Robertshaw et al., 1978; Simon, 1981; Salthe, 1985; Warfield, 1973; Baldwin, 1975; Optner, 1965). Particular attention is paid to how complexity and uncertainty affect the environmental problem-solving process.

ESSENTIAL STUDY ELEMENTS

Attempts to solve irrigation-induced water quality problems—whether the problem is related to selenium, boron, a pesticide, or something else—cannot succeed unless the process used to identify, evaluate, and eventually implement the responses is sound. In its guidance to the U.S. Department of the Interior and the SJVDP, and by this report, this committee continually has emphasized the need for formal decisionmaking and effective public participation in this process, and it has stressed the importance of carefully integrating technical, socioeconomic, and institutional considerations.

Certain key study elements are critical when decisionmakers attempt to seek balanced solutions to significant environmental problems. In general, problem-solving endeavors such as the SJVDP and the National Irrigation Water Quality (NIWQP) should incorporate the following five basic elements:

1. Recognize the problem.
2. Define the problem.

3. Assess the data base and collect additional data.
4. Identify alternative responses.
5. Evaluate the alternatives.

Table 4.1 summarizes the general process that needs to be followed to generate responses to major environmental problems when values, viewpoints, and science may be in conflict. The process begins with the antecedent conditions that set the stage for the occurrence of a problem. These antecedents are the environmental variables that create the setting. As was reviewed in Chapter 2, they can include the hydrologic or geologic characteristics, ecological or biological factors, or other physical elements that characterize the existing conditions. In addition, as was reviewed in Chapter 3, the social and cultural context—the economic, social, and political setting—also creates a backdrop against which a problem occurs. These elements all contribute in various ways to the complexity of the problem and the ultimate effectiveness of various proposed solutions.

In the San Joaquin Valley, for example, two of the most important antecedents were the geology of the area (i.e., the fact that the soils were rich in selenium) and the nature of the agricultural economy (i.e., the history and importance of irrigation in the valley). If either of these two variables had been different, the problem at issue would not have occurred or at least would have been significantly different.

As was mentioned earlier, defining the problem is a critical and difficult step in the problem-solving process. Implementation of any solution is impossible if people do not agree as to the nature of the problem (Vlachos et al., 1979), because how the problem is defined ultimately determines the nature of the solutions that are possible. Of course, difficulties arise because different people have different perspectives and thus will define different problems. The compromise is to define the problem broadly and then specify concrete, feasible goals that serve, as best possible, the different perspectives. Rarely, if ever, is it possible for all parties to be fully satisfied, and some value judgments will have to be made.

Ultimately, one clear problem must be defined—a process that may involve some difficult value judgments—because without this basic understanding, obtainable goals cannot be set and alternative solutions cannot be analyzed in context. If the problem-definition process is adequate, in the end local, regional, and national interests should be appropriately balanced.

Table 4.1 also lists categories of available responses. These are the generic tools available to address irrigation-induced water quality problems anywhere, whether in the San Joaquin Valley or elsewhere in the United States or the world. They are basic types of responses that might be applied regardless of site. These can be technical, institutional, or a combination of both approaches. Appropriate responses can be developed only after

TABLE 4.1 General Process for Developing Strategies to
Respond to Irrigation-Induced Water Quality Problems

Sequence of Steps	Essential Components
Recognizing the problem	Detection of anomalies o Chemical parameters o Physical parameters o Biota o Social impacts o Economic impacts

Defining the problem,
  assessing and collecting data
	Antecedent conditions
	o Hydrological
	o Biological
	o Geological
	o Ecological
	
	Social and Cultural Context
	o Historical setting
	o Competing and conflicting
	    demands
	o Inherent complexity
	o Widespread support for irrigated
	    agriculture
	o Subsidization of water and crops
	o Expectation of continued support
	o Institutional constraints

Identifying alternatives	Possible responses o Source control o Drainage water treatment o Transport and disposal o Price adjustments o Legal changes o Institutional changes o Economic changes o Social changes
Evaluating alternatives	Criteria for evaluating responses o Technical soundness o Economic viability o Legal appropriateness o Social acceptability o Political feasibility o Ecological appropriateness

careful interpretation of the data. These responses are discussed further in Chapter 5.

Given the dynamic nature of any problem-solving process, one cross-cutting issue critical to the search for appropriate responses is public participation. Public participation is important throughout the various stages of any problem-solving endeavor, but it is particularly necessary during the definition of the problem and the assessment of alternative responses (Ingram and Ullery, 1977). In fact, the success of any proposed solution will ultimately depend on the public's confidence that the decision process was open and complete. Public participation is important because it is inevitable in any large, public debate that there will be differing views present among the people affected. In other words, there is no one "public" but rather many "publics" that must be given access to the decision-making process: farmers (both irrigators and nonirrigators), business people, environmentalists, local and regional residents, and a host of others with varied rationales for involvement. All sides desire a chance to be heard and to share in the decision-making responsibilities.

Public participation brings competing interests together, communicates information, identifies research needs, and helps in the understanding of scientific uncertainty. It is a forum for decision makers and the public to listen and learn from each other. Public participation is not a frill; it is a necessity that has been established by law and upheld by the judiciary. Thus the question is no longer whether there should be public participation, but how it can be done most effectively.

Recognizing the Problem

The first step toward solving a problem is recognizing that it exists. Although problem recognition is difficult and often occurs by happenstance, examples of strategies to facilitate problem recognition include the baseline monitoring of chemical and physical parameters as conducted by the U.S. Geological Survey, remote-sensing efforts by the National Aeronautics and Space Administration and the National Oceanic and Atmospheric Administration, and isolated long-term ecosystem monitoring efforts supported by the National Science Foundation. Many of these efforts are designed primarily to explore the long-term behavior of natural systems. The number of parameters monitored often is small, and the geographical coverage of the studies is limited.

Monitoring detects change. Defining change in the natural world as a problem, no matter how the change is discovered, depends on a value judgment by some part of society because damage is a human value concept. Science can serve society through sustained research vigilance, but the decision determining which changes are problems (damage) requires close coordination between monitoring and evaluation.

Two common shortfalls interfere with many schemes for problem recognition. One difficulty occurs because the scientific and technical programs charged with monitoring generally are separated from the value judgment methods that could identify a change as damage. The second difficulty is that the technical institutions responsible for monitoring are often the same institutions responsible for causing the changes, often in the name of resource development. This creates a built-in bias to ignore unintended problems as long as the original objectives of the projects are being met.

Few formal strategies exist for efficient problem recognition covering a wide range of circumstances. Consequently, many problems are first recognized through dramatic, attention-getting events such as the deaths and deformities of birds at Kesterson National Wildlife Refuge (NWR), or through serendipity during studies designed for other purposes. Thus the threshold of severity that must be reached before a problem is recognized can vary significantly. The first indications that a problem may exist tend to be based on the following:

- inferences drawn from prior experiences;
- detection of anomalies in chemical or physical parameters;
- detection of anomalies in the biota; or
- detection of socioeconomic impacts.

Many of the potential problems uncovered during the problem-recognition phase will turn out to be spurious, and therefore such associations need to be assessed carefully to enable judging the strength of the association and the likelihood of causal relationships. Again, the San Joaquin Valley offers a vivid example of how problem recognition can occur: because the selenium contamination at Kesterson NWR was unexpected, the mass media played an unprecedented role in the problem-recognition process.

Given the experience gained at Kesterson NWR, monitoring for trace elements at other sites may be better able to detect emerging problems when the changes are more subtle and before drastic problems have arisen.

Defining the Problem

The next critical step in solving any problem is to define the nature of the problem (Box 4.A). Problem definition for complex, multidisciplinary environmental problems requires agreement among competing interests. Developing a process to negotiate an acceptable statement of the problem is a necessary part of problem definition and should precede the setting of goals.

The importance of an interdisciplinary team undertaking a formal

---

BOX 4.A   Defining the Problem

It is important to negotiate an acceptable problem definition early in any research effort because different observers will have different perspectives, focus on different symptoms, and have different goals. The views expressed can vary widely. A farmer may see the problem as one of diminishing agricultural productivity, and the causes as increased salinity, rising water tables, diminished irrigation supplies, or contaminated irrigation water. A water resources management agency may see the problem as the excessive accumulation of harmful pollutants in the hydrological system. An environmental activist may focus on the loss of natural environmental attributes caused by the expansion of agricultural systems. The impacts of diminished in-stream flows on aquatic wildlife, recreation, and drinking water supplies, or the simple degradation of natural landscapes, can also be issues.

From a national perspective, the major problem may be the significant costs required to maintain the current agricultural system. Over the years, the nation has developed an agricultural production system which, on the one hand, appears to be very efficient in producing plentiful supplies of inexpensive commodities, but which, on the other hand, requires billions of dollars of subsidies for its maintenance. Other people will identify still other types of problems. And even within any general problem area, different individuals may define the problem differently.

All of these different definitions have some credibility. And indeed, the full definition of "the problem" may include elements of all the different definitions and more. But all too often, little attention is given to defining exactly what the problem is, and this failure will often become a major cause of subsequent confusion and conflict among those responsible for identifying a solution.

---

problem decomposition was discussed above. The problem-definition phase defines the purpose of the research and the future outcome that is desired. The participants must resist the urge to find quick solutions during the problem-statement phase. Sometimes a team of experts with no vested interest in the outcome—in other words, a panel of outside experts—is best suited to evaluate the problem objectively. In any event, the inclusion of formal value judgment is required.

It is absolutely essential to define a problem before seeking to solve it. Although this may sound simple or obvious, it is not. When asked to specify the problem they are trying to solve, farmers, scientists, engineers, citizens, federal and state agency staff, and other interested parties may all see the problem differently or may focus on different symptoms. Public participation must be incorporated at this early stage of problem definition. Acknowledging the existence of different views of a problem is important because it means that the problem solvers will be less likely to proceed down a short-sighted path.

How the problem is defined—whether explicitly or implicitly—will determine which options are examined and implemented. Obtainable goals can be set only if the problem to be solved is clear and agreed upon by all parties. Different options will produce different effects on the various interest groups. A response at the local level may aggravate the problem at the state or national level. The simplest engineering response may be an environmental mistake. A temporary remedy may preclude a future, permanent cure. The benefits of each alternative for all affected parties must be carefully assessed, and decisionmakers must remember that all potential solutions have costs—in money, resources, energy, and social costs. Who will pay becomes an essential consideration, and, as for the other questions raised, the answer depends very much on the perspective from which the question is asked. It may be that no answers are possible in which all the parties win, so that compromise is more often than not the only realistic goal.

This committee cannot stress enough the importance of clearly defining exactly what problem is being addressed and of making early problem definition a crucial element in all attempts to study and solve irrigation-induced water quality problems in the future. Each level of a problem contains its own set of intertwined subproblems. If certain elements of the problem are ignored, unforeseen repercussions will result. For example, plugging the drains that discharged into the ponds at Kesterson NWR was a response that did reduce the flow of contaminants into the refuge. However, it did not solve several larger problems, such as what should be done with the sediments that contain dangerous residues or who should pay for cleanup. It did not address the obvious question of how to maintain agricultural production without drainage, or the more subtle question of how to compensate for the wetland habitats that were lost.

Data Assessment and Acquisition

Assessing the Data Base

Once a problem has been defined and goals set, problem solvers should next assess the existing data base (National Research Council, 1986; Larkin, 1984). Too often, people confronted with a complex problem tend to assume that the required data are absent and immediately begin acquiring new data. Existing data often are ignored, underused, or treated as suspect. Although existing data may have been developed from studies with different objectives, they still can provide valuable insights about the nature of the system interactions, a key component when dealing with complex problems.

From the existing data base, researchers should attempt to establish a baseline, a trend, and some idea of the required endpoint. The question of how (by what criteria) to judge the problem must also be addressed. The research team should first screen the facts. This involves separating objective information from expert opinions, educated guesses, speculations, and other questionable data. But this step inevitably includes some value judgments, and these opinions need not be discouraged; they simply need to be noted for what they are.

The assessment of quantitative and qualitative information derived from ecological field studies is particularly difficult to deal with because such studies often exhibit poorly quantified precision and accuracy. Nevertheless, such studies may be the only ones that integrate the effects of combined stresses on the environment. A well-designed exploratory analysis of the existing data base can help decisionmakers assess the quality of this data base and identify significant data gaps. If the facts are insufficient, further information must be acquired.

Before acquiring new data, however, problem solvers need to develop a formal statement of the specific measurement objectives, including a complete list of variables to be measured. The reporting units, expected ranges, required detection limits, relative prediction (upper limit), and accuracy (maximum absolute bias) objectives must be specified for each target parameter before measurement begins. Clearly stated data objectives are necessary to the design of a quality assurance and quality control procedure at the beginning of the measurement process (Box 4.B).

Often a quality control plan is developed too late to be of real use in assessing the quality of information being acquired. A clear statement of data objectives also helps field and laboratory personnel assemble candidate measurement procedures and examine their cost-effectiveness. Questions of sampling strategy, definitions of sample representativeness, and similar issues all require specific objectives. Attention to method selection, development, and optimization should precede the adoption of routine analytical measurement procedures. Appropriate laboratories and investigators must also be selected to perform the work.

Acquiring Additional Data

Existing data can provide important input into the decision-making process, but they will likely need to be supplemented with new data specifically tailored to the situation. Thus data acquisition is a key, and often time-consuming, stage in environmental problem solving. One area of particular importance is public health. The potential threat to public health posed by the increasing exposure of people and wildlife to water contamination mandates a closer examination of the importance of these data.

BOX 4.B　Quality Assurance and Quality Control

Uncertainty plays a constant and important role in problem solving. To properly evaluate alternatives, a quantitative mechanism for monitoring uncertainties should be included in all experimental designs. The design of a quality assurance (QA) plan and implementation of quality control (QC) procedures should occur early in any study. A member of the study team should be assigned responsibility for QA/QC. When a project incorporates the work of many people in several places, a QA/QC manager should be appointed as early as possible. In addition to the manager's coordinating role, several broad QA objectives can be addressed only by a QA/QC manager. Establishing QA program guidelines for data precision, accuracy, completeness, representativeness, and comparability requires a whole-project perspective that individual participating laboratories and data-gathering task groups cannot provide.

Decisions about the utility of data for answering particular questions depend on the objective of the study, the sampling design, and protocol. There are data adequate to answer some questions that would be useless for answering others. In addition, the degree to which one may assess sample representativeness depends on the precision limits of the analytical methods, i.e., whether field variability may be distinguished from laboratory imprecision. Thus, once the goals for analytical precision have been established, one may define representativeness and establish a protocol for assessing whether the objectives have been achieved. If this is carefully done and meticulously documented, then future analysts can be confident that data are, or are not, appropriate for new analyses. These are important criteria for long-term data sets that must serve time series analyses, analyses of change, and analyses about the effects of experimental manipulation or management.

In particular, monitoring, dose response studies, and exposure assessments (Box 4.C) play a key role in risk assessment and in the evaluation of alternative responses to a problem.

Monitoring, or the routine collection of data, is used in ecological studies in two basic ways. Anticipatory monitoring is designed to track the effects of activities that might be cumulative or pose hazards to human health. Monitoring during or after an action or project is designed to show what ecological changes resulted (Baker, 1976). Properly done, monitoring provides continuous indexes of environmental quality that can signal environmental degradation or improvement (National Research Council, 1986).

Monitoring often is avoided because it is expensive and the return of information for each dollar spent seems small. The additional expenditure may be difficult to defend because the contribution that monitoring data

---

BOX 4.C   Exposure Assessment

Exposure assessment is a process used to estimate the rates at which substances are absorbed by organisms through all mechanisms: ingestion, inhalation, and by absorption through the skin. The absorbed dose often differs significantly from the dose externally applied to the organism, which is usually called the exposure.

A valid measurement of the organism's exposure to a chemical would require measuring that chemical in the food, drinking water, air, and surfaces with which the organism would come into contact. Environmental concentration measurements that do not consider the chemical and physical forms of the contaminants provide an imperfect basis for estimating absorbed doses because these forms affect the gastrointestinal absorption efficiency, the percutaneous transfer coefficient, and other important parameters. Ideally, the analytical data should also provide information on the physical and chemical form of the substance being analyzed. In practice, most exposure assessments do not incorporate such sophistication, and the resulting environmental assessments are weak.

When a possible environmental contamination problem is initially investigated, a large number of potential contaminants should be sought in those areas where they would be expected to accumulate, by natural processes, to unusually high concentrations. Next, the team should clearly define the geographical extent of the problem and the major environmental media for those contaminants uncovered in the preliminary phase. Then the team should concentrate on making exposure measurements for humans and selected organisms. Monitoring data collected during reconnaissance should not be used to make definitive risk assessments without clarifying the tentative nature of such assessments.

---

provide to assurance of safety and effectiveness generally is not evident during the initial years.

Monitoring is, however, quite important during all phases of a water resources investigation, and its importance will increase as water quality problems become more frequent and the sources of contamination more abundant and diverse. Survey monitoring, for example, tracks ambient conditions, detects changes, and identifies problem areas on a routine reconnaissance basis. As anomalies are detected, it may be necessary to supplement existing monitoring networks with additional measurements to obtain a better understanding of the study system.

Monitoring should not be restricted to the period of study of a particular problem situation but should be continued after packages of solutions have been selected and implemented. This continued monitoring provides a means to assess the effectiveness of the strategic response chosen and permits identification of other potential anomalies. Of course, one serious problem in designing any monitoring system is the assumption that someone knows what substances to monitor. Had a well-designed water monitoring system existed in the San Joaquin Valley prior to the discovery of problems at Kesterson NWR, it probably would not have provided advance indication of the selenium contamination because there was no basis in experience that warned researchers to monitor explicitly for selenium.

The National Irrigation Water Quality Program (NIWQP)—the creation of which was inspired by the San Joaquin Valley experience—provides an example of the kind of basic data collection and monitoring that is necessary to identify irrigation-related contamination problems. This program is an attempt to anticipate and identify contamination problems before they take on Kesterson-like proportions, and it relies on a series of evaluative steps ranging from desk reviews to reconnaissance-level field studies to detailed field studies at sites showing potential problems. Given that the nation now is aware of these types of problems and their potential consequences, this committee believes some program of this type will remain necessary in the long term.

Interpreting the Data

Converting the assembled data into information is as important to problem solving as experimental design is to data gathering. One element of any information-gathering process should be an information base management system. The data acquisition/interpretation plan supplies an operational mechanism for information exchange and catalyzes the interdisciplinary interaction. Interdisciplinary research requires a concerted effort to force researchers to address the data/information base in its broadest interpretive context.

A well-designed information management system should be more than just computer software or a commercial data management system. It should incorporate human creative elements using interpretive aids to display the data conveniently, summarize its information, induce thinking about its content, and facilitate its use as an instrument of reasoning. The data base manager is a key individual in the interdisciplinary team. The individual should have the technical expertise needed to critically evaluate the data and function as an aid to retrieval and analysis. All projects benefit from the broader perspective of a competent generalist. Thus one central role for information management is to provide the day-to-day continuity that keeps the systems design approach productive. Chapter 5 addresses data interpretation in more depth, as it is fundamental to the tasks of identifying and evaluating alternative responses and strategies.

COMPLEXITY AND STUDY DESIGN

Many descriptions of environmental problems begin by stating that the problems are complex. Although this may appear to be a statement of the obvious, study designs seldom exhibit a truly thoughtful examination of the claimed complexity. Irrigation-induced water quality problems are indeed complex. But one central role for natural science is "to show that complexity, correctly viewed, is only a mask for simplicity" and "to find pattern in apparent chaos" (Simon, 1981). The solutions to complex problems are not always themselves complex, although they must take into account the relevant complexity. Complexity can be addressed through study design. Two types of complexity—descriptive and interactive—need to be considered.

Descriptive Complexity

Descriptive complexity results from observers with different perspectives and institutions with different missions using different approaches to dissect a system into subsystems (Box 4.D). This often results in poor problem definition, and one consequence of this is that too much time is spent trying to solve the wrong problems. Descriptive complexity occurs because inherent differences of scale—whether spatial or temporal—are addressed differently by individuals with differing objectives. For example, a farmer whose objective is economic survival will describe a problem in a more short-term light; a resource manager, given a mandated responsibility for the resources being managed, is likely to describe the complexity more broadly in terms of both time and space.

The difference in the perception of beneficial or adverse effects also varies given the perspective—environmental, agricultural, or societal. To accommodate descriptive complexity, dynamic and flexible approaches to problem solving are necessary. The approaches must be interdisciplinary and must involve the public.

The distinction between "interdisciplinary" and "multidisciplinary" is more than semantic. Simply including studies from several disciplines does not ensure that relevant system interactions will be uncovered or that integrative, interpretive solutions will be obtained. Humans are adept at recognizing complexity but often avoid implementing remedies that require widespread changes in behavior. The complexity itself becomes an excuse for lack of action. This makes problem definition and planning key steps in problem solving.

Complex problems often have a hierarchical structure, and solutions require the use of formal systems analysis. Systems are collections of things that function together, and the study of these collections is called systems

---

BOX 4.D   Descriptive Complexity in the San Joaquin Valley

Some of the complexity that characterizes the situation in California's San Joaquin Valley came about because events inevitably mixed together people who held incompatible values. Different people express their goals in different terms: tons of cotton, waterfowl, human health, money, influence, or esthetics. Thus the San Joaquin Valley case is also a "complexity of values," generally expressed as special interests.

Nowhere was the potential for conflicting perspectives more apparent than in the seemingly simple task of exactly defining the problem in the San Joaquin Valley. Is the principal issue how to better manage water on the farm so that the volume of drainage, and thus contaminated waste water, is minimized? Or is it how to protect water quality and in-stream values? Is the question one of broad economic benefits for the nation, or of continuing the historic agricultural lifestyle in the San Joaquin Valley? Is the issue the protection and enhancement of wildlife resources, particularly waterfowl habitats? Are the events in the valley an isolated problem or are they representative of a broad national issue?

These questions reflect the different perspectives, levels of authority, and interests of the many people involved and potentially affected by the answers. Local governments often perceive the issues much differently than do federal agencies. In fact, although many institutions exist to examine separate pieces of the water use puzzle, none has shown the breadth and flexibility needed to integrate water policy across the disciplines.

---

analysis (Haith, 1982). There are obvious advantages in treating environmental problems as systems. Problems can be considered in their totality, and the most effective points of control can be sought. A consequence of a systems perspective on environmental quality is the broadening of possible control options and subsequent opportunities for efficient, integrated management strategies (Haith, 1982).

A formal, collaborative systems analysis can help identify the levels of the problem hierarchy and provide a useful mechanism for breaking down the problem into its essential elements. This decomposition allows the various parts of a complex system to be considered in isolation, but still in the context of the whole. Decomposition makes it easier to identify any part of the problem that needs particular attention, and it is easy to put things back together when the decompositions are formal. This is how science seeks to simplify.

The levels of the hierarchy are characterized by shared properties, such as spatial scale and temporal frequency, each subject to different degrees of resolution during data collection phases of empirical science (Box 4.E). Formal examination of the levels of the hierarchy permits the

---

BOX 4.E   The Problem Hierarchy in the San Joaquin Valley

When a problem is analyzed, spatial resolution determines how much area is examined and temporal resolution determines the length of time. Three geographic scales are obvious in the San Joaquin Valley example: Kesterson National Wildlife Refuge (NWR), the San Joaquin Valley, and the arid West. Three time scales are appropriate: short term (years), medium term (decades), and long term (centuries). Cleanup at Kesterson NWR represents a local, short-term goal. Reassessing water management in the San Joaquin Valley addresses a watershed on the medium term. Achieving a balance between sustainable agriculture and environmental values would be a long-term goal.

A hierarchy of problem levels is clearly present. The discharge of drainage water into the ponds at Kesterson NWR has left a serious toxic cleanup problem; this is commonly referred to as the "Kesterson problem." Second, the plugging of the contributing drains has aggravated drainage problems for much of the irrigated land on the west side of the San Joaquin Valley, and this is referred to as the "San Joaquin Valley drainage problem." Third, the documentation of toxic concentrations of selenium in the drainage water raises the spectre of similar problems elsewhere in the West, and this broad issue is called the "irrigation-induced water quality problem."

It is easy to see how these differences in perspective add to complexity. The drainage problems in the San Joaquin Valley have been examined according to a variety of different organizational strategies. Economists, politicians, ecologists, and legal analysts each simplified the issues by assuming that the others' views were fixed. The extradisciplinary information then was included as a constant or discarded as irrelevant.

---

problem-solving team to identify essential communication channels in the interdisciplinary structure.

Many disagreements, particularly those that are hard to settle, are characterized by the disagreeing parties having addressed the issue at different levels, or in different contexts, with different values influencing their perspectives.

Such disagreements are not resolved by factual information. When it is realized that no answers are possible in which all parties win, the establishment of a common ground followed by compromise becomes the only realistic goal. In essence, there are no win-win situations, only compromises in which all parties must give a little to attain a solution acceptable to all. The systems approach to problem solving provides a rubric for such problem definition and a structure for interdisciplinary collaboration.

Interactive Complexity

While descriptive complexity is the result of problem perception, interactive complexity is characteristic of natural systems. It is the result of direct or indirect interactions among variables within a subsystem or of interactions between subsystems. For example, the question of cadmium toxicity to humans cannot be adequately addressed without understanding the status of zinc. The toxic interaction between these two elements is mediated by natural biochemical processes occurring in human cells. Most environmental problems contain many significant interactions. Thus an engineer, chemist, or biologist might view complexity in terms of the number and magnitude of system interactions. Unless these interactions are identified and understood, the solutions proposed are likely to fail.

In a complex problem the relevant complexity must be accounted for, but the key to useful solutions is to reject the irrelevant complexity and uncertainty. It has become all too common to claim that "everything is connected," but good study design reflects the fact that most things can be looked at separately and that most connections are weak and can be ignored. On the other hand, it is essential to recognize and deal with significant interactions and to be aware that the sum of a number of weak interactions may be significant. It would be an error to think that when a dominant cause has been identified, the other factors are irrelevant. Thus a good study design should create a data-gathering structure that is capable of discovering unanticipated interactions and determining the magnitude of expected interactions. Failure to adequately address interactional complexity during problem definition leads to short-term solutions that can be long-term disasters.

In addition to variable interactions within a domain of study, interactions between domains also introduce complexity that must be addressed in a study design. Although adequate theory may exist to predict interactions within a study domain, theory that identifies and permits quantitative assessment of interactions between apparently disparate domains is lacking. For example, interactions between elements of the technical domain and the social and economic domains—that is, the linkages between science and values—are poorly understood. Furthermore, few theoretical constructs exist to link phenomena occurring at different scales. This means that predictability at large scales (regional, continental, or global) or far into the future is not yet possible.

UNCERTAINTY

Given a good problem representation and a recognition of relevant interactions, the problem solver must then map the consequences of the alternatives, recognizing that some predictions will be more certain than others. Thus, to understand the nature of complexity and its consequences in a problem-solving endeavor, the problem solvers must examine the role of uncertainty.

Since the consequences of actions may be far reaching and long lasting, a predictive capability is useful for assessing the effects of human activity. Accurate prediction, however, requires a theoretical understanding of the phenomena to be predicted as well as reliable data. Unfortunately, available scientific theories often are incomplete, and the available data are uncertain. Successful problem solving must be based on a strategy that addresses complexity and recognizes that uncertainty is an inherent part of any problem.

Uncertainties can be of two types: those that people know how to remove without extraordinary effort, and those that people do not know how to remove without extraordinary effort or that may not even be recognized in the problem.

The first type of uncertainty includes the random errors associated with measurement, and measurement limitations imposed by methods with insufficient sensitivity, data gaps, and so on. Although sometimes problematic, these can be minimized without too much effort. If these uncertainties cannot be ignored, then problem-solving procedures must determine the added cost of reducing the uncertainty to acceptable levels and must compare that cost with the cost of not having the additional information. For example, improving the measurement precision by a factor of two could easily increase the cost of the measurement by a factor of four. It is not always clear that the reduced uncertainty in a few measurements will proportionally improve the final uncertainty in complex systems. In any case, quantitative information regarding the measurement process and continuous performance surveillance are essential parts of problem solving. The crucial role of a quality assurance and quality control program will be described in more detail below.

The second type of uncertainty deals with uncertainties that arise out of science's incomplete understanding of how things work. Uncertainties of this type include the variabilities of human behavior, the weather, political events, and similar factors where judgments are based on assumptions rather than facts. Even with extraordinary efforts, these uncertainties cannot be modeled adequately. Hidden variables perturb the system in unanticipated directions, which makes prediction very uncertain even when the uncertainties related to measurement type have been minimized.

Since these uncertainties arising from exogenous events cannot be quantified, attempts are made to deal with them by estimating the probabilities that they might occur (another assumption) using risk analysis (Tardiff and Rodricks, 1987; Hogan and Hoel, 1989), as highlighted in

---

BOX 4.F   Risk Assessment

Risk assessment is a process that seeks to estimate the likelihood of occurrence of adverse effects due to specific exposures to chemical, physical, and biological agents in humans as well as ecosystems. The assessments may involve qualitative as well as quantitative estimates. Risk assessments often must be made from fragmentary data and with data that were collected for purposes not related to making risk assessments. Thus, by their very nature, risk assessment processes emphasize extrapolations and are sometimes prone to inaccuracies.

Risk assessment is but one phase in a much larger process that seeks to prevent adverse effects on public health or ecosystems or the economy. It is closely linked with exposure assessment and with risk management. Risk management combines political, legal, and engineering approaches to manage risks.

Potential risks are estimated by considering the probability of occurrence, the potential effects, and the exposure, all in order to make the assessment of potential risks associated with the exposure to chemicals more tractable. There are, however, generic limitations to risk assessment. For instance, the number of substances for which an adequate amount of information exists for credible risk assessments is limited. Risk assessments for complex mixtures and for intermittent and fluctuating exposures are unreliable. Risk assessments for the protection of ecosystems are only in their early developmental stages.

Box 4.F. Risk analysis, based as it is on assumptions, contains significant uncertainties. An alternative or supplementary uncertainty management strategy is to build feedback controls into the study design and solution implementation plan so that plans can be altered as data improve or as more is learned about the system.

The three elements outlined here—recognizing a problem, defining the problem, and assessing the data base and collecting additional data—are essential steps in any problem-solving endeavor. To identify appropriate responses—ones that adequately and fairly respond to the stated goals of the problem-solving endeavor—requires careful analysis. Technical, economic, legal, ecological, social, and political criteria must all be evaluated in an attempt to weigh the relative advantages and disadvantages of each proposed approach. The identification and evaluation of appropriate responses is of course the cornerstone of any problem-solving endeavor. These critical steps receive detailed attention in Chapter 5.

CONCLUSIONS

Environmental quality problems tend to be complex, difficult to resolve, and controversial. However, a problem's complexity should not be an excuse for taking no action to solve it. A substantial degree of formality will be necessary to address complex problems successfully. This will help reduce wasted effort, increase the scientific integrity of the process and the solutions ultimately proposed, and foster their public acceptance.

When designing studies to resolve environmental problems, it is important to recognize the nature of complexity—both to acknowledge it and to remove the excuse that, because of the complexity, the problem is intractable. The hierarchical nature of a large, complex problem involving many disciplines and interest groups must also be recognized because communication is possible only at the same hierarchical level.

A well-conducted study plan employs, in order, the elements of problem recognition, problem definition, data assessment and collection, generation of alternative solutions, and evaluation of these alternatives. In structuring any study, explicit attention must be paid to quality assurance and quality control, data and information management, monitoring, risk assessment and uncertainty, public participation, and conflict management. One aspect of complexity is that no environmental problem is solely technical or solely institutional in nature. All involve technical, legal, social, and institutional components.

A formal systems analysis framework will aid in giving appropriate weight to each of these disciplines and in enhancing communication. A wide range of alternative potential solutions needs to be displayed and analyzed formally. This not only avoids the obvious pitfall of overlooking important possibilities, but it also provides a basis for establishing the costs of the preferred alternatives compared to others. It also increases the credibility of the study recommendations.

As indicated in Chapters 2 and 5, the solutions to most environmental problems will involve important technical components. However, such solutions cannot be solely technical but rather must also deal in legal, social, economic, and institutional domains, as emphasized in Chapters 3 and 5. These components should be integrated throughout the problem-solving process. Viable long-term solutions must be chosen based on societal judgment, and these can be assessed only when accurate information on the economic, legal, and institutional environment is available.

REFERENCES

Baker, J. M. 1976. Biological monitoring—principles, methods and difficulties. In Marine Ecology and Oil Pollution. J. M. Baker, ed. John Wiley & Sons, New York.

Baldwin, M. M., ed. 1975. Portraits of Complexity: Applications of Systems Methodologies to Societal Problems. Battelle Memorial Institute, Columbus, Ohio.

Haith, D. A. 1982. Environmental Systems Optimization. John Wiley & Sons, New York.

Hogan, M., and D. Hoel. 1989. Extrapolation to man. Pp. 879-891 in Principles and Methods of Toxicology. 2nd Ed. A. Wallace Hayes, ed. Raven Press, New York.

Ingram, H. M., and S. J. Ullery. 1977. Public participation in environmental decision-making: substance or illusion. Pp. 123-139 in Public Participation in Planning. W. R. D. Sewell and J. T. Coppock, eds. John Wiley & Sons, New York.

Larkin, P. A. 1984. A commentary on environmental impact assessment for large projects affecting lakes and streams. Can. J. Fish. Aquat. Sci. 41, 1121-1127.

National Research Council. 1986. Ecological Knowledge and Environmental Problem-Solving: Concepts and Case Studies. National Academy Press, Washington, D.C., pp. 104-115.

National Research Council. 1987. River and Dam Management: A Review of the Bureau of Reclamation's Glen Canyon Environmental Studies. National Academy Press, Washington, D.C.

Optner, S. L. 1965. Systems Analysis for Business and Industrial Problem Solving. Prentice-Hall, Englewood Cliffs, New Jersey.

Robertshaw, J. E., S. J. Mecca, and M. N. Rerick. 1978. Problem Solving: A Systems Approach. Petrocelli Books, New York.

Salthe, S. N. 1985. Evolving Hierarchical Systems: Their Structure and Representation. Columbia University Press, New York.

Simon, H. A. 1981. The Sciences of the Artificial. MIT Press, Cambridge, Massachusetts.

Tardiff, R. G., and J. V. Rodricks, eds. 1987. Toxic Substances and Human Risk. Plenum Press, New York. 445 pp.

Vlachos, E., G. V. Skogerboe, G. E. Radosevich, P. C. Huszar, and W. Trock. 1979. Socio-Economic and Institutional Factors in Irrigation Return Flow Quality Control. Prepared for Robert S. Kerr Environmental Research Laboratory, Office of Research and Development, U.S. Environmental Protection Agency (EPA Grant R-8034742).

Warfield, J. N. 1973. An Assault on Complexity. Battelle Memorial Institute, Columbus, Ohio.

5
Resolving Problems:
Identifying and Evaluating Alternatives

The ultimate goal of the problem-solving process discussed in this report is to select and implement responses to help reduce or solve irrigation-induced water quality problems. The problem-solving process described is one that can be applied broadly to the nation's environmental problems. Regardless of the specific circumstances, however, one step in this process merits special emphasis: identifying and evaluating the full range of alternative solutions available.

Chapter 4 outlined the generic systems approach necessary to assess any complex environmental problem and discussed the first steps of such a process. This chapter concentrates on the final steps—identifying and evaluating the range of responses available to decisionmakers.

This committee has emphasized just how important it is for decision makers to display and debate openly the full range of available alternatives before filtering this broad group to a subset of most appropriate options. No potential option should be dismissed a priori, even if intuition judges it to be impractical or unpopular.

In conceiving alternatives, there is a tendency to restrict the range of alternatives considered for two reasons: first, the people developing the list may have backgrounds that steer them to consider approaches within their expertise and leave them biased against "unconventional" solutions, and second, some obvious alternatives may be rejected a priori because they are assumed to be impractical, legally difficult, or politically unpopular. This tendency to prejudge—or to fail to recognize—a number of alternatives must be overcome. As with problem definition, the judgment of a team of outside experts without vested interests can be useful in providing fresh insights and ideas.

A few examples may illustrate the issue, even if their simplicity appears to overstate the point. The mission of the U.S. Bureau of Reclamation has been to develop water resources for irrigation. In searching for solutions to irrigation-induced problems, its personnel historically have not been likely to seriously consider reducing or eliminating the use of irrigation. Ocean disposal of irrigation drainage water, as another example, has been restrained by laws and regulation. Those accustomed to operating within the rules may not appreciate that laws can be changed; an academic scientist, on the other hand, is likely to see ocean disposal as a natural process, only accelerated by irrigation. This outside vision might recognize the value of assessing the costs, benefits, and disadvantages of various means of ocean disposal. Fish and wildlife specialists are accustomed to being last in line when it comes to water resource allocations. They may not appreciate that water for wildlife purposes might be provided at the upper end of an irrigation scheme, prior to use for irrigation, rather than at the lower end, after degradation.

Thus, a wide range of alternatives—structural and nonstructural, technical and institutional—should all be displayed and openly debated. These also should consider shifts in priorities or shifts in the end use of the resource. Identifying and evaluating a full range of options should ensure that innovative ideas are not prematurely eliminated and that the true costs and benefits of each of the options can be assessed.

To ignore certain options—whatever the reasons for doing so—is to jeopardize the credibility of the overall analysis. Obviously, in the latter stages of any study the time and energy spent on the various options will begin to be weighted in favor of the more appropriate options (after all, this is the point of the study and evaluation process), but this should never preclude the importance of giving all options equal consideration in the early stages of an analysis.

Using irrigation-induced water quality problems as a focus, the two sections below list selected classes of options to demonstrate the range that must be considered. One section discusses technical responses and the other discusses institutional responses, even though it is clear that successful strategies will need to combine elements from both categories. No attempt is made to be exhaustive or to advocate any particular option. Specific action packages from this range can only be chosen deliberately on a case-specific basis, and they must incorporate the essential elements of good problem solving described in Chapter 4.

TECHNICAL OPTIONS

The irrigation of arid lands brings about major changes in land use and in the distribution and use of water. This in turn leads to a redistribution of salts, with unintended and sometimes unanticipated consequences. These impacts of redistribution often are minor initially, but they tend to become increasingly important over time.

The primary and long-recognized adverse effect of irrigation is the generation of drainage water that carries substantial amounts of salts. The more acute and less common effect, vividly illustrated in the San Joaquin Valley, is the mobilization of specific trace elements in relatively small, but potentially toxic, concentrations. In evaluating drainage options, this distinction between types of problems must not be lost. A response that may be feasible for selenium removal may not be applicable for boron or nitrate removal. A treatment for a specific trace element may have no application for total salt load management.

The redistribution of salts is a universal feature of irrigation in arid lands, and many of the problems associated with irrigation are due to excessive salt concentrations. Thus the long-term viability of irrigated agriculture becomes a matter of "salt management"— devising strategies to prevent salts from accumulating either in the irrigated area or downstream.

The basic approaches available for this task include transporting the salts out of the system and storing salts where they will do no harm, leaving the salts in place, or treating the drainage water. Retiring problem lands from irrigated agriculture is an example of an approach directed at leaving salts in place. Deep-well injection is an example of storing salts, while building drainage canals to take the salts to the ocean is a means of exporting them. The following sections explore these classes of options in more detail.

Through most of history, the most common approach to salt management on irrigated lands has been to discharge drainage water into streams. In the process, the often highly concentrated drainage waters are diluted by mixing with the river flow so that no adverse environmental effect is noted immediately. While this process has been used many times in many places, the cumulative effect can be severe, especially if it is combined with water diversions from the river. In fact, in principle, concentration is desired to reduce the cost of handling the waste stream and to reduce the volume of water dedicated to the disposal process.

Transport and Disposal of Drainage Water

The primary objective of draining irrigated lands is to remove excess water and salts in order to maintain a root environment suitable for crop growth. However, once the drainage water has been collected, the salts must be transported and disposed of in some acceptable manner—by dilution or by storage in a location where they will cause little damage. Treatment of the drainage water may also be necessary to facilitate either transport or disposal.

Ocean Disposal

One direct way to dispose of drainage water is to discharge it to the ocean. The challenge is to avoid adverse effects in transit. In some cases, salts in the discharged water can be sufficiently diluted with other water so they do not create a water quality problem during transport. This traditional approach has often been carried out by constructing drainage canals to carry drainage water either back to a river with enough dilution water in it, or directly to the ocean. If the salts do not ultimately reach the ocean, however, the water quality problem is only being postponed or moved elsewhere. For instance, the disposal of the return flows from the New Lands Project into the Truckee River in Nevada has only served to cause severe water quality problems in the Stillwater basin.

Studies assessing disposal of the San Joaquin Valley's drainage water by discharging it into San Francisco Bay or directly into the ocean have shown these options to be expensive and controversial. As indicated in Chapter 1, the San Luis Drain originally was to extend to the bay, but its high construction cost and public opposition resulted in its being terminated in the ponds at Kesterson National Wildlife Refuge (NWR). Although the planners had hoped that additional funds would be allocated to complete the drain, such a solution is probably no longer socially or politically acceptable because of concerns over possible adverse impacts on water quality at the point of discharge.

Another ocean disposal option would be to transport the San Joaquin Valley's drainage water directly to the ocean through closed conduits constructed over the Coast Range. This approach would be expensive and also has generated substantial opposition.

Taking the analysis beyond the example in the San Joaquin Valley, it must be recognized that ocean disposal generally involves transporting drainage water in natural channels (e.g., the Colorado River). The question to be answered regardless of site is whether a management plan can be devised that avoids or reduces adverse effects associated with transport and discharge.

Deep-Well Injection

Another technology undergoing study is deep-well injection, when excess salts are disposed of by injecting them into abandoned deep wells

(Lee et al., 1988b). Deep-well injection has long been used by the oil and gas industry to dispose of oil field brines. The application of this technology for agricultural drainage water is a relatively recent modification, however, and it faces a variety of technical, financial, and institutional constraints.

For instance, because of the great volume of drainage involved, it may not be feasible to inject the entire return flow, requiring first that the drainage be treated to reduce the volume and as a consequence concentrate the salts. This would be an expensive undertaking. If the entire return flow were injected, substantial amounts of water would be removed from possible use by downstream residents or to support in-stream flows. Furthermore, it is difficult to establish with certainty that the injected water will not have long-term negative effects on regional water quality. Also, there is some concern that large volumes of injected water could destabilize the region tectonically.

Source Control

Source control can be described as those salt management activities that are undertaken at the farm level, the source of the drainage water. Salt management approaches that rely on source control essentially rely on leaving the salts on the land.

Retirement of Land from Irrigated Agriculture

One way to manage salt loads is to retire the most problematic lands from irrigated agriculture. Land retirement eliminates the need for salt and water disposal on those lands retired. As a result of reducing the number of acres irrigated, the rate of export of salts offsite through ground water and surface runoff also is reduced. Alternate land uses chosen for the retired acreage must be assessed to ensure that water use and drainage volumes would be reduced.

Management of Irrigation

Another approach to managing salts at their source is through irrigation management. The quantity and quality of irrigation drainage water can be affected significantly by increasing the efficiency of irrigation by better management of existing systems or by introducing more advanced irrigation technology (van Schilfgaarde et al., 1974). One example of a technologically advanced system enabling precise control of water application is subsurface trickle irrigation with automatic feedback control for determining the timing and amount of water application. Such systems are designed to reduce drainage while increasing water use efficiency and crop yield, but at a relatively high cost of capital investment and management skills (Phene et

One technical approach for managing salts at their source is through improved irrigation management. Drip irrigation, used here on furrowed cotton in California, conserves water and energy and reduces the threat of erosion. Such systems can reduce drainage but are expensive and require increased management skills. Inset: close-up of an "in-line" emitter. CREDIT: Soil Conservation Service, T. McCabe.

al., 1988). Such techniques can reduce drainage volumes well below 10 percent of the amount of irrigation water applied.

One approach is to recycle drainage water and use it directly, perhaps diluted and supplemented with additional irrigation water, to grow salt-tolerant crops. Rhoades et al. (1988) demonstrated that as much as 50 percent of the water used to irrigate crop rotations that included cotton, alfalfa, melons, and sugar beets could be supplied from a drainage source containing over 3000 mg/l total dissolved solids. This option, however, may simply transfer increasing salinity problems to sites downstream.

Irrigation management alone will not provide a long-term solution to salt management but can delay the onset of a problem until other approaches become more feasible. It can retard the rate of salt discharge in the drainage water and, at a steady state, often reduce the total mass of salts discharged. In addition, irrigation management simultaneously reduces the amount of drainage water that ultimately needs to be removed. Unlike land retirement, irrigation management allows agricultural production to continue. However, source control activities generally require more careful

Throughout history, the main challenge for irrigated agriculture has been salt management. Evaporation ponds are a commonly used means to deal with saline subsurface drainage water, but the potential for adverse environmental impacts is significant. The light-colored areas in cropped fields are due to high soil salinities resulting from poor drainage.
CREDIT: Jim Oster, University of California, Riverside.

management than is necessary with more traditional irrigation techniques, and they result in higher salt concentrations in the drainage water.

Onsite Evaporation Ponds

The major mechanism available to concentrate salts is evaporation, a process seen throughout the arid West in naturally formed salt lakes and dry salt beds. The construction of onsite evaporation ponds to collect and concentrate salts from irrigation water drainage is an attempt to use this natural process to store salts temporarily or permanently at a selected location. Evaporation ponds are a commonly used means to deal with saline subsurface agricultural drainage water (Lee et al., 1988a). Although many drainage dischargers view ponds as a viable means of disposal, the potential for adverse environmental impacts is significant.

One disadvantage of evaporation ponds is that the area devoted to the ponds is removed from agricultural production or other uses for the foreseeable future. Typically, 15 percent of the land area farmed must be sacrificed to the pond (Tanji et al., 1985). Another is that evaporation ponds remove water from the system and thus reduce the amount available to downstream users and for in-stream flow.

Evaporation ponds can be biologically productive and attractive to waterfowl. The biological productivity can be expected to decrease, however, as the salt concentration increases. Also, unless specific measures are taken to prevent the seepage of saline waters into ground water, evaporation ponds also can contaminate local ground water. However, after evaporation ponds have been in use for some time, the ponds tend to seal, substantially reducing saline water intrusion into the ground water.

The presence in the drainage water of trace elements, even in relatively small quantities, changes the situation drastically. Concentration through evaporation can lead, in short order, to levels that are toxic to fish and fowl. In fact, in the San Joaquin Valley, excessive levels of arsenic, boron, molybdenum, and selenium have been noted in some evaporation ponds (Schroeder et al., 1988). Such ponds are no longer just evaporation ponds, but need to be considered as potentially hazardous waste disposal sites, subjecting them to stringent regulations.

Extensive studies of both the biological and chemical characteristics of evaporation ponds where trace elements are a problem have led to design recommendations intended to reduce the ponds' use by biota. Multicell ponds with a minimum water depth of 1 m, with steep sides, and with banks and levees cleared of vegetation will reduce use by waterfowl, shore birds, and macroinvertebrates. Aquatic plants can be controlled with herbicides, and other pesticides may be needed to control invertebrate populations (Parker and Knight, 1989). In short, this presumably simple solution to a waste disposal problem can readily grow into an expensive and environmentally hazardous endeavor that may no longer be called a solution.

Thus onsite evaporation ponds can offer only an interim service that can be useful while other, permanent solutions are sought. They will also, however, create a new range of problems in the long run.

Drainage Water Treatment Technologies

Scientists and engineers have developed a number of water treatment technologies that might be applied to irrigation-related problems. Some are applicable to specific substance removal; others remove all salts. These technologies are, in general, an expensive approach to salt management. They also add the problem of disposal of the removed salts.

Desalinization Technologies

Desalinization technologies usually are used to create high-quality water, usable for drinking or other purposes, from a saline source. The primary technologies used in desalinization are reverse osmosis and flash evaporation. Both are capital and energy intensive, and thus the cost of separating the salt from the water tends to be high. A desalinization plant is being built near Yuma, Arizona, to remove salts from the Wellton-Mohawk Irrigation and Drainage District before the drainage water is released to the Colorado River. However, analyses show that this is a very expensive option (van Schilfgaarde, 1982). The use of such technologies also creates the problem of disposing of the highly concentrated salt-rich waste. Thus these technologies only provide ways of concentrating the mixture to be disposed of; they are not a solution to the problem itself. Desalinization plants need to be part of an integrated strategy for residual salts management.

Chemical and Biological Removal

Chemical and biological approaches can also be used to address some salt management issues. In the San Joaquin Valley, for instance, high concentrations of selenium are of special concern. Studies have shown that ferrous ions or iron filings can be used to create selenium-rich sludges that can be separated from the drainage water (Lee et al., 1988a; Murphy, 1988). However, even if one of these processes were perfected and made economically attractive, it would still leave two problems. First, the total salt concentration would not be affected and the need would remain to dispose of the selenium sludge. Second, these approaches are specific to selenium and do not address the wider question of other trace elements.

One biological approach investigated in the San Joaquin Valley uses fungi to remove selenium. Certain fungi, when provided with a source of energy and maintained in a favorable (anaerobic) environment, will metabolically convert selenium compounds to volatile dimethyl selenide (Lee et al., 1988a). This process shows potential to remove selenium from contaminated soils (Frankenberger and Karlson, 1988). Again, however, this approach is selenium specific.

Another proposed biological approach that deals specifically with selenium involves using organisms that facilitate selenium accumulation in biota without causing toxic responses (Lee et al., 1988a). In small pilot projects, bacterial filters have demonstrated some success, but the feasibility of this approach at a large scale is uncertain, and it is doubtful that the technology can be worked out in the short time frame necessary for remediation.

The biologically oriented technologies that show some promise have not advanced past the research or pilot stage. If found to be feasible, they would need to be evaluated as part of an overall management strategy.

INSTITUTIONAL OPTIONS

Finding a solution to the complicated water quality problems caused by irrigation requires a careful review of institutional as well as technical options. Although the two options are addressed separately in this chapter, they cannot be dealt with separately in actual practice. As was discussed in Chapter 3, the social and scientific aspects of a problem are inextricably intertwined. In many cases, an institutional option would be used to bring about the use of a preferred technical option. Ultimately, the finest technical option is of little value if there is no institutional way of assuring its implementation and continuing operation.

Situations exist where institutional change alone might bring about desired improvements. Even if no specific technical option is preferred, adopting certain institutional changes can encourage irrigators to adopt one or more of several beneficial options. The choice is left to the individual decisionmaker, depending on the particular circumstances.

The strategies ultimately chosen to cope with irrigation-related problems will undoubtedly involve a mix of various institutional options. This section discusses four types of institutional options: price adjustments, legal changes, organizational changes, and political and social changes.

Price Adjustments

Chapter 3 discussed the various economic factors that contribute to the water quality problems associated with irrigation drainage water. Many of these problems occur because the prices irrigators pay for their resources or receive for their products do not reflect actual social costs. Thus one way to correct these discrepancies is to adjust the relevant prices.

Accurate Market Prices

The most obvious discrepancy is in the price that irrigators pay for irrigation water. Adjusting the price of water so that irrigators pay the full cost of providing it would make those farmers served by government irrigation facilities operate more efficiently. In situations where irrigation proved to be an uneconomic operation, it would reduce the amount of irrigated acreage. Irrigators would tend to use less water, thus leaving more to serve other social purposes. Even a relatively small reduction in demand would free significant water supplies for other uses because of the substantial amount of water consumed by irrigated agriculture in western states.

Similarly, removing price supports for surplus crops would induce irrigators to grow fewer of these products, again resulting in an increase in efficiency and a reduction in government price support payments.

However, such changes, as much as they might improve the system's general efficiency, are unlikely to correct drainage problems fully. They might reduce the amount of drainage generated, but they would not necessarily reduce it in those areas causing the most serious problems. Making such major price changes could also significantly worsen the financial condition of many farmers and cause other unwanted social repercussions. Many of the people affected would not be causing downstream water quality problems. Others would find it more difficult to invest in alternative actions to reduce drainage problems. Finally, as simple as such price adjustments appear in theory, they would be difficult to implement. Many irrigators obtain their water under long-term contracts in which the prices already have been established. For irrigators who provide their own irrigation supplies, the only way to adjust the cost of water is for the state to charge for the right to use water. Although such charges are not unknown, they would represent a radical change and would be hotly resisted.

Similar implementation problems affect proposals to remove price supports from irrigated crops. There would be no effective way to implement such a policy unless the supports were eliminated for all farmers. Nor would such a change necessarily have a significant impact on irrigation drainage problems.

Taxes and Charges

One way to adjust costs in a manner more closely focused on drainage problems is to impose taxes or charges on the irrigators responsible for these problems to pay the costs of ameliorating the damages. Special drainage taxes could be instituted for problem lands or inputs such as water, fertilizers, or pesticides in problem areas. Economic theory suggests that increasing the effective price of these inputs would induce some farmers to conserve them.

Practical problems arise, however. It may not be legal or possible to focus taxes on inputs used only in specific drainage problem areas. Furthermore, input taxes are not necessarily an efficient approach to solving environmental problems caused by output (e.g., drainage). However, this approach has the benefit of providing a source of revenue that could be used to fund mitigation programs.

Alternatively, irrigators could be charged on the basis of the amount of drainage they generate or the amount of contamination in that drainage. Such charges (or effluent fees) might act to induce irrigators to take actions to reduce the volume of drainage or the quantity of harmful constituents in the drainage.

Charges on outputs also provide the advantage of generating revenue. Again, however, this approach would be difficult to implement, particularly in irrigated areas where drainage is difficult to measure because it occurs underground in natural channels rather than in constructed networks.

Subsidies

Another way to adjust prices is to subsidize those investments or other purchases that the government wants to encourage. Such subsidy programs are particularly common in the agricultural sector. The government often shares in the cost of soil and water conservation measures on private farms or provides free services such as education and extension. In other sectors, tax benefits and tax-free bonds may be more common types of subsidies.

Subsidies have the advantage that they can be focused on the most serious problem areas. Subsidized technical assistance, for instance, can be focused on the farms thought to be creating the most serious problems. Extension agents can work directly with farmers to identify the most effective means of eliminating problems at a given site. If a proposed solution involved some investment (e.g., the installation of a more efficient irrigation system), the government might also share in its cost. Cost-sharing is generally more difficult, although not impossible, when the response involves improved management practices.

The major difficulty with subsidies is that they require increased government expenditures for a sector that is already heavily subsidized. Adding additional subsidies may only increase overall inefficiencies. Furthermore, the subsidies typically are available only for certain types of activities, and these are not always the most effective or efficient solutions.

It is possible, however, to use subsidies in conjunction with regulatory procedures. The Food Security Act of 1985 introduced the principle of cross-compliance: farmers' eligibility for various support payments was made contingent on their adoption of conservation practices. Similar cross-linkages between good management practices or drainage reduction on the one side, and subsidized water prices or crop price supports on the other, may offer an opportunity for persuasion without excessive unilateral controls.

Legal Changes

Existing legal provisions strongly influence the feasibility of selecting various technical solutions to reduce the water quality problems associated with irrigation drainage water. In some cases, modifying these provisions to remove certain constraints could help in the implementation of desired solutions. However, it is also possible that new laws may have to be enacted to authorize a preferred approach.

Constraints on Water Transfers

Both state and federal laws and procedures significantly affect the economic benefits and costs associated with market transfers of water rights (Colby, 1988). Some improvements in the efficiency of irrigation systems could be accomplished by addressing these legal constraints. Perhaps the most important of these would be modifying existing provisions for selling water rights. Although they vary from state to state, existing provisions often provide no incentive for irrigators to use water more efficiently because they are unable to sell the water that is conserved. State policies that allowed conserved water to be applied to new land and new uses and that allowed conserved water to be leased or sold would reward conservation efforts and could reduce disincentives for water conservation generated by forfeiture and abandonment laws (Saliba and Bush, 1987).

At this time, laws in the western states vary considerably. In Arizona, while no specific statutes regulate the transfer of conserved water, case law seems to preclude transfers to lands other than those to which the water right was originally assigned. California, on the other hand, specifically provides that conserved water may be sold, leased, or otherwise transferred. Nevada law takes the position that "since beneficial use is the limit and extent of a right, a water user has no right to his inefficiencies." Thus conserved water is considered unappropriated and any applicant may file to appropriate it (Saliba and Bush, 1987).

As was discussed in Chapter 3, the question of who actually owns the rights can also be complicated. In some cases it is the irrigator, in some cases the irrigation district, and in some cases the U.S. Bureau of Reclamation (USBR); in some cases ownership may not be clear. Even if state law supports efficient water transfers, federal authorizing statutes or the USBR's administrative procedures may inhibit such an approach.

Reducing the constraints on water transfers would not, by itself, necessarily reduce the water quality problems associated with irrigation drainage. In a manner similar to increasing water prices, it could lead to a general improvement in the efficiency with which water is used, but these improvements would not necessarily be focused on areas creating the most serious water quality problems. However, if the preferred technical solution involves improved water management or taking certain lands out of production, easing the irrigator's ability to sell the water saved could significantly encourage implementation.

Constraints on Drainage

Existing water law also could be modified to make it pertain to the quality of the drainage water as well as to the quantity withdrawn and consumed by irrigators. At the federal level, abolishing the section of the Clean Water Act that exempts irrigation return flows from the pollution control provisions governing other dischargers might be the most direct approach. Similar changes could be made in state water quality laws. Such changes, however, would retain the existing separation between the legal structure governing water quantity and that governing water quality.

Incorporating water quality concerns directly into the legal structure governing the allocation of water would probably require states to modify their existing legislative doctrines. Conceivably, the reasonable use doctrine could be expanded to include a water quality dimension, for instance by declaring that reasonable use requires that any unused water or waste water be of sufficiently good quality that it causes no damage to downstream users or to the environment. Such a concept is at least implicitly incorporated in the riparian doctrine of water use but historically has had little influence on the quality of water discharges in areas where that doctrine prevails.

Another approach might be to expand the concepts incorporated in the public trust doctrine to include water quality concerns. This doctrine was used by the California Supreme Court to control the amount of water that Los Angeles could remove from the Mono Lake basin because of the impacts these withdrawals were having on the water quality in Mono Lake and on the viability of the ecosystem. This doctrine, however, is not clearly defined, and how it might be applied to any particular circumstance is very uncertain.

Regulatory Approaches

The most direct legal approach would be to adopt new regulatory programs that would require the implementation of desired technical solutions in those areas causing significant water quality problems. These programs could control any or all stages of the irrigation and farming process: the use of inputs, irrigation management, or the quality of the drainage.

Controls on inputs could limit which lands are irrigated, restrict the amount of irrigation water applied to the land, or restrain the types or quantities of agricultural chemicals used (if these are the cause of the water quality problem). However, controls on inputs may not solve the problems and are likely to be inefficient. One method proposed to control agricultural use would be to define soils containing trace elements in problem-causing quantities as "geologic hazard areas" and restrict agricultural use that would cause leaching and deep percolation. This could be legally similar to existing floodplain management strategies.

Controls on irrigation management could include any of the techniques described previously in the "Technical Options" section of this chapter. Again, adopting such a regulatory approach implies that the regulator knows how to solve the problem as well as or better than the individual farmer. In some cases, it can be difficult to enforce this type of approach because of the difficulty of determining whether the farmer is in fact using the required management practice.

Controls on the quality of the drainage water or on the ambient quality of the receiving water focus most directly on the problem of concern and allow the irrigator the most flexibility in choosing how to solve the problem. However, enforcing such an approach can be a problem because of the difficulty and cost of monitoring drainage flows. Controls on ambient quality also raise questions about allocating responsibility for the problem among the various dischargers.

One possibility might involve raising the level of control from the individual irrigator to the water district. This could reduce the need for intensive monitoring and quantitative source determination at the farm level by passing the responsibility of allocation to the members of the district. This issue is addressed further in the section "Organizational Changes" in a somewhat different context.

Organizational Changes

Implementing effective and efficient solutions to the problems being experienced in the San Joaquin Valley may require modifications in certain administrative organizations because of the conflicting responsibilities of the different agencies and institutions involved in water management.

Broadening and Redefining Responsibilities

One way to reduce the institutional problems caused by conflicting responsibilities would be to broaden the responsibilities of existing institutions. For instance, water supply institutions such as the USBR and the water (and irrigation) districts could be made responsible for the quality of drainage water as well as the provision of water for irrigation. Alternatively, water pollution control agencies could be given responsibility for supplying water as well as controlling the amount of pollution in water discharges. The geographic jurisdiction would have to be defined along hydrologic boundaries rather than political ones.

If a major effort were made to broaden some agency responsibilities, some conflicts and confusion would likely result because several different agencies could then have responsibility for dealing with the same problem. Thus there would need to be a concurrent redefining and consolidating of agency responsibilities. These changes would probably be very difficult to implement. They might, however, help significantly to prevent future problems such as the contamination of Kesterson NWR. They also might improve the nation's capability to respond to those problems that have already occurred if they ultimately helped improve coordination and communication among the nation's water resource and water management agencies.

Correcting Other Institutional Impediments

In the process of attempting to deal with the problems at Kesterson NWR and similar sites throughout the West, numerous other institutional constraints will undoubtedly be discovered. Problems involving the length of irrigation contracts and the question of who actually owns water rights have already been mentioned.

Another institutional impediment in some parts of the San Joaquin Valley is that water often is delivered to irrigation districts and individual farmers on a fixed schedule, regardless of whether it is needed. This can result in the farmer applying excess water to the land, thus causing increased drainage. Such a system also precludes the farmer from adopting efficient irrigation systems that apply low volumes of water on an almost continuous basis. A water delivery system set up to make water available when it is needed would reduce these problems and would probably increase production and improve water use efficiency. Such a change, however, would require investments to increase the capacity of water supply systems and to provide nearby storage facilities.

The types of changes needed to resolve such institutional constraints will depend on the technical solutions that are selected. For some technological choices, institutional constraints may be very important; for others, the significance may be less.

Finally, the search for the best solution must recognize that different agencies and institutions are governed by different legal standards and follow different administrative procedures. Some of these standards and procedures may be too ponderous to allow an agency to respond effectively to the problems associated with irrigation drainage water. Thus the institutional procedures governing the institution itself can constitute an important consideration when an institutional response is selected.

Political and Social Changes

No technical or institutional solution, no matter how elegant, is likely to be implemented successfully if it does not have adequate political and social support from all sides of the controversy. This is one reason why the entire process of identifying and evaluating alternative solutions should be open and should involve substantial public participation. Active efforts need to be made to build support for the desired changes in the state and federal legislatures as well.

One primary consideration in developing social and political support for a proposed solution is how the costs and benefits are distributed among the affected populations. If this distribution is seen as inequitable, significant opposition can develop. Finding the "right" balance can be one of the trickiest parts of deciding on a solution. If it offers powerful political interests too few benefits, or if they are expected to pay what they perceive as an undue portion of the costs, they may be able to block a proposed solution politically. However, significant opposition also can result if less powerful interests such as small farmers or minorities are unfairly affected, or if the general taxpayer is expected to pay a major portion of the bill for investments that will benefit a small group of already heavily subsidized irrigators.

EVALUATING ALTERNATIVES

The final step in the study process is to evaluate the technical and institutional options that have been identified and select those that appear to be most attractive. Although this is the final step in the study process, the criteria and procedures that will be used need to be clearly thought out and made explicit at the beginning of the study. If this is not done, the prior steps may not provide the information necessary to conduct solid evaluations, and the evaluations and ultimate decision may be considered suspect.

Thus much of the planning for the evaluation phase should be conducted early in the study, most appropriately at the time that the problem is being defined. Like the problem-definition process, this planning should incorporate substantial public input and discussion. All segments of the public need to have confidence that the decision-making process is legitimate and that it will reflect their values. Making an effort to build this confidence at the beginning of the process should help the entire study proceed more efficiently and should result in the final recommendations being broadly supported. It is an investment that is usually very profitable, but all too rarely made.

Thus the committee cannot overemphasize the importance of defining the problem clearly and comprehensively. How the problem is defined—whether explicitly or implicitly—will determine what solutions are explored and implemented. Obtainable goals can be set only if the problem to be solved is clear and agreed upon by all parties. All responses have different impacts on the affected interest groups. A response at the local level may aggravate the problem at the state or national level. The simplest engineering response may be an environmental mistake. A quick fix may preclude a future, permanent cure. The benefits of each alternative for all affected parties must be carefully assessed, and decisionmakers must remember that all responses have costs—money, resources, energy, and social costs. Who will pay becomes an essential consideration, and, like the other questions raised, the answer depends very much on the perspective from which the question is asked. It may be that no answers are possible in which all the parties win, so that compromise is more often than not the only realistic goal.

Evaluation Criteria

The principal evaluation criterion is, of course, the extent to which the proposed option will help solve the problem the study is addressing. Again, this emphasizes the importance of defining the problem accurately and early. The link between problem definition and the ultimate choice of options can be solidified by including in the definition explicit measures for determining how success will be measured. For instance, if the problem is defined to be deteriorating water quality, the definition of the problem should indicate which particular contaminants are of concern (e.g., selenium alone, other specific salts, all salts, all agricultural chemicals, all contaminants for which water quality standards are in place, or some other specific list of substances). The definition should also indicate whether improvement would be measured by the average concentration of pollutants in the receiving water, the maximum concentration of pollutants in the receiving water, or some other criterion.

Success in solving the defined problem is not, however, the only criterion for evaluating alternative options. Various other technical, economic, institutional, and environmental criteria must also be considered.

In the water resources field, substantial effort has been spent over the past 40 years developing criteria and procedures for project evaluation. These were first compiled and published in the *Federal Register* in 1973 (Water Resources Council, 1973). This landmark discussion of principles and standards set forth four "accounts"—national economic development, environmental quality, social well-being, and regional development—that are to be evaluated when analyzing the advantages and disadvantages of proposed water resources projects supported by any federal agency. An update published in 1983 provides additional principles and guidelines (Water Resources Council, 1983). The regulations implementing the National Environmental Policy Act's requirement that environmental impact statements be prepared for such projects, and Executive Order 12291, which requires that cost benefit analyses be conducted for many federal activities, also influence the structure and content of evaluation processes carried out for federal actions.

Regardless of the particular requirements or emphases of these specific evaluation procedures, any comprehensive evaluation should consider four general categories of criteria—technical, environmental, economic, and other institutional. Again, the way in which these evaluations will be conducted and the specific criteria and measurements that will be used in the evaluation process should be spelled out early in the study process.

Technical Criteria

Any proposed response to an irrigation-induced water quality problem needs to be technically and scientifically sound. Where the technology has been proven and widely demonstrated to be effective in real applications, the primary concern is whether there is anything different about the proposed application that might disrupt the technology. For new technologies, however, the evaluation will need to consider whether the technology acts in concert with scientific principles, whether it is consistent with existing engineering practice, whether it is likely to have any adverse side effects, and whether there are any characteristics of the proposed application that might interfere with its functioning properly.

Any technology ought also to be evaluated on the basis of whether it truly resolves or only changes the problem, and whether the solution is long term or short term. A technical approach that simply removes the salt from the drainage water (e.g., using a membrane desalinization process) has a disadvantage; although it may remove the contaminants from the water, it creates another waste stream of high salt concentration that still requires disposal. Some solutions, such as the original proposal to use Kesterson NWR to evaporate irrigation drainage water, may work in the short term but be ineffective or even create more serious problems in the long term.

Environmental Criteria

Although the environmental and ecological viability of proposed activities often was not given significant consideration in the past, this has now become a primary concern. At the least, the proposed action should have little adverse impact on the stability and functioning of existing natural ecosystems. Beyond being environmentally nondamaging, however, responses that help restore degraded ecosystems and increase the provision of environmental amenities are generally to be preferred over those that do not.

Evaluating the absence of negative impacts and the provision of environmental benefits needs to be closely tied to the technical analysis and evaluation of the option. Otherwise the technical analysis may miss some potentially significant impacts, and the project design may miss some important opportunities to generate environmental benefits.

The environmental evaluation is often difficult for two reasons. One is the often substantial uncertainty involved in efforts to assess and predict environmental effects. The second is the problem of developing good, unambiguous measures of these effects.

Economic Criteria

The third set of criteria relate to the economics of the proposal. Economic efficiency is usually a major consideration. Is the proposal cost-effective—that is, does it represent the least-cost way of achieving the benefits it provides? How efficient is it—that is, by how much do the expected benefits exceed the expected costs? These are the standard questions regarding the proposal's economic efficiency.

But economic efficiency is only one aspect of the economic evaluation. A second is the financial question—is the proposal affordable? Particularly in times of tight government budgets, very expensive projects are unlikely to be funded even though they appear to be very efficient. No matter how efficient a proposal may appear in theory, the concept has little meaning if the project is never implemented.

Another important economic consideration is how the benefits and costs of the proposal are likely to be distributed. Who will end up paying for, and who will end up receiving, the benefits? Is this distribution equitable? Is there any way of getting the beneficiaries to pay more of the costs? This distribution question will be closely tied to the financial question of how the proposal will be funded.

Other Institutional Criteria

All proposed alternative responses also must be evaluated in light of various other institutional criteria such as social and political acceptability, whether the responses are in accord with existing laws and court interpretations, and whether they fit into existing institutional responsibilities.

The more congruent the proposal is with existing practices, the more likely it is to rate well according to these criteria. On the other hand, however, environmental problems are often caused by existing practices; when that is the case, any effective solution will have to change those practices. The questions then become how much the practices have to be changed, how difficult these changes will be, and what incentives can be created to encourage them.

The fundamental question in this part of the evaluation is whether the proposal can actually be implemented. The most effective and efficient approach is of little value if it cannot (or will not) actually be put in place.

In this case, the evaluation phase may involve significant effort to develop effective implementation strategies. An assessment of the likely success of these options should then be fed back into the technical, environmental, and economic evaluations to develop improved estimates of how well the proposal will in fact address the problem.

Clearly there are very few ways of quantitatively measuring these institutional criteria. That fact, however, does not diminish the importance of their evaluation.

The Evaluation Process

Evaluation—the analysis and interpretation of data—is required for understanding. Careful thought is necessary to turn data into information. The interpretive activities that facilitate the conversion of data into information are seldom given sufficient attention in study design.

Programs of the magnitude required to solve environmental problems must establish a specific plan to evaluate and interpret the data. Researchers should not expect that some obvious answer will emerge on its own or that the measurements acquired by the individual disciplinary team members will be integrated for effective interdisciplinary problem solving without pointed efforts. Serious effort is necessary to transform data into relevant information.

Although the evaluation process is the last to be completed, it should not wait until all the other study elements are accomplished. Instead, the evaluation process should be ongoing. Nor should every proposed response necessarily receive the same thorough analysis. Relatively simple evaluations conducted early in the study may demonstrate that some options are clearly undesirable, for instance because they are technically infeasible or prohibitively expensive. Thus the evaluation process may be a series of evaluation filters, with increasingly rigorous analyses being conducted as the study progresses.

Another reason for beginning these analyses early is that they may demonstrate that some important questions are not being asked or necessary information is not being collected. Thus there should be feedback from the evaluation phase to the information-collection phase. The feedback can also occur in the opposite direction if information collected in other phases of the study indicates a need for modifying evaluation criteria—for instance, by adding additional contaminants or considering additional environmental effects.

The process of investigation, analysis, and evaluation of alternatives is dynamic. Judgment must be exercised in a process that weighs criteria, constraints, and opportunities and that uses comprehensive, interdisciplinary analysis to generate a variety of possible appropriate responses.

To determine the appropriate responses, decisionmakers should assess how the various actions respond to the goals articulated early in the problem-solving endeavor. In most cases, a combination of approaches will be necessary.

Four sources of input need to be weighed in the decision-making process, including:

1. technical input and scientific standards;
2. legal mandates and administrative guidelines;
3. political input; and
4. public desires (which sometimes can differ dramatically from political input).

In the past, professionals with relevant technical expertise tended to make most resource management decisions. Over time, however, the U.S. legal system has evolved to provide broader guidance, and the public has become increasingly involved. Also, it was assumed in the past that the public view was represented by the political input, but that perception has now become more realistic.

The identification and evaluation process must consider questions such as the following:

- Does the option involve proven technology?
- What are the costs, and what are the benefits?
- Who pays, and who benefits?
- How difficult is it to implement the option?
- What is the time frame—is the option a temporary or a permanent solution?

What emerges from a constructive consideration of these questions will not be one "right" solution but rather a combination of institutional initiatives and technical measures. In the process of formulating this mix, trade-offs associated with different options will become evident. Legal or political constraints will emerge that might interfere with the implementation of some options that may appear technically attractive.

The final decision will involve a difficult process of weighing competing and conflicting demands and developing procedures to alleviate or manage the conflicts. Trade-offs must be recognized and compromises negotiated. Each stage in a problem-solving endeavor should involve some effort to consider equity questions—basically, who pays and who benefits. An effective solution cannot be implemented without weighing the trade-offs that are inherent in any judgments and choices. Resolving disputes early in the process reduces the probability that the courts will need to play a role later in the process. In the end, the ultimate decision on what actions to take to reach the stated goals will be a compromise blending technical and institutional components.

CONCLUSIONS

Chapter 4 introduced five basic functions that characterize problem solving: (1) recognizing a problem, (2) defining the problem, (3) assessing the data base and collecting data, (4) identifying alternative responses, and (5) evaluating those responses. Although these discussions have focused on independent system components, the importance of an interdisciplinary approach cannot be overemphasized. The ultimate task in problem solving is to evaluate the information gained for each component in relation to the others and to integrate that information for interpretation. Thus the final function to consider in any problem-solving endeavor is how to use an iterative process incorporating these basic steps.

As data are gathered and evaluation proceeds, a series of possible responses will evolve—some with less certain outcomes than others. While some types of uncertainty can be dealt with explicitly and quantitatively through good quality control, other types of uncertainty can only be handled through the adoption of compromise. The goal of using an iterative problem-solving process is to provide feedback for midcourse corrections, so that control can be exercised even when the events cannot be predicted.

In the management of natural resources, the ecosystem processes that are being managed occur on time scales longer than the design of most experiments. The areas being managed typically are large. It follows, therefore, that knowledge from experimental science at these scales is likely to be sparse. Monitoring can be thought of as the straightforward data-collection phase of long-term, large-scale experiments. Monitoring plays a crucial role in evaluating and assessing the success (or lack of success) of management in meeting stated goals.

Because a system's response to management at these scales is not likely to be perfectly predictable, and because, as a system changes in response to management, predictability may be even less certain, it may be necessary to alter management strategies as data become available. A mechanism for continuously reevaluating the data and information base in light of emerging alternative responses needs to be formalized. This evaluation should determine how well management goals are being achieved so that alterations in the whole problem-solving and data-gathering process can be implemented.

Another crucial aspect of the iterative process involves analyzing the full range of possible alternatives, including those that appear to warrant further attention as well as those that appear flawed. This is helpful to the long-term success and eventual public acceptance of the chosen option. An analytical methodology to identify the diverse and often conflicting environmental and economic considerations can be developed through iterative reevaluation. It aids in identifying and quantifying diverse elements. Iteration also provides a process for presenting relevant information and mechanisms for compromise (making the necessary trade-offs). The public is more likely to have confidence in the final decisions if they are made in a logical and open manner, following a process that has been carefully thought out and subjected to public review.

REFERENCES

Colby, B. G. 1988. Economic impacts of water law—state law and water market development in the southwest. Natural Resources Journal 28, 721-749.

Frankenberger, W. T., Jr., and U. Karlson. 1988. Dissipation of Soil Selenium by Microbial Volatilization at Kesterson Reservoir. Final report, Project 7-FC-20-05240. U.S. Department of the Interior, Washington, D.C.

Lee, E. W., G. H. Nishimura, and H. L. Hansen. 1988a. Agricultural Drainage Water Treatment, Reuse, and Disposal in the San Joaquin Valley of California, Part I: Treatment Technology. Technical report, San Joaquin Valley Drainage Program, 2800 Cottage Way, Rm. W-2143, Sacramento, California.

Lee, E. W., G. H. Nishimura, and H. L. Hansen. 1988b. Agricultural Drainage Water Treatment, Reuse, and Disposal in the San Joaquin Valley of California, Part II: Reuse and Disposal. Technical report, San Joaquin Valley Drainage Program, 2800 Cottage Way, Rm. W-2143, Sacramento, California.

Murphy, A. P. 1988. Removal of selenate from water by chemical reduction. Ind. Eng. Chem. Res. 27, 187-191.

Parker, M. S., and A. W. Knight. 1989. Biological characterization of agricultural drainage evaporation ponds. Water Science and Engineering Paper No. 4521. Department of Land, Air, and Water Resources, UC-Davis. 51 pp.

Phene, C. J., K. R. Davis, R. L. McCormick, and D. Heinrick. 1988. Subsurface Drip Irrigation: Management for Maximizing Yields and Reducing Drainage. Proceedings of Drip Irrigation Symposium, San Diego, California, pp. 34-54.

Rhoades, J. D., F. T. Bingham, J. Letey, A. R. Dedrick, M. Bean, G. J. Hoffman, W. J. Alves, R. V. Swain, and P. G. Pacheco. 1988. Reuse of drainage water for irrigation: Results of Imperial Valley study I. Hypothesis, experimental procedures and cropping results. Hilgardia 56(5), 1-16.

Saliba, B. C., and D. B. Bush. 1987. Water Markets in Theory and Practice: Market Transfers, Water Values, and Public Policy. Westview Press, Boulder and London, pp. 64-65.

Schroeder, R. A., D. U. Palawski, and J. P. Skorupa. 1988. Reconnaissance investigation of water quality, bottom sediments, and biota associated with irrigation drainage in the Tulare Lake bed area, southern San Joaquin Valley, California, 1986-87. U.S. Geological Survey, Water Resources Investigations Report 88-4001. U.S. Geological Survey, Books and Open File Reports Section, Denver, Colorado.

Tangi, K. K., M. E. Grismer, B. R. Hanson. 1985. Subsurface drainage evaporation ponds. California Agriculture 39(9 and 10), 10-12.

van Schilfgaarde, J. 1982. The Wellton-Mohawk dilemma. Water Management and Supply 6(1/2), 115-127.

van Schilfgaarde, J., L. Bernstein, J. D. Rhoades, and S. L. Rawlins. 1974. Irrigation management for salt control. J. Irrig. Drain. Div., ASCE 100(IR3), 321-338.

Water Resources Council. 1973. Establishment of principles and standards for planning water and related land resources. Federal Register, Vol. 38, No. 174, Part III, September 10.

Water Resources Council. 1983. Economic and environmental principles and guidelines for water and related land resources implementation studies. U.S. Army Corps of Engineers, Department of the Army, Circular No. 1105-2-115. 137 pp.

6

Recommendations

In undertaking this report, the National Research Council's Committee on Irrigation-Induced Water Quality Problems sought to provide a discussion of the insights gained from the San Joaquin Valley experience and to highlight some lessons that should not be overlooked when similar environmental problems arise in the future. The committee attempted to focus on questions of a long-term, interdisciplinary nature—ones that address the national public interest—and it wishes to remind scientists, resource managers, politicians, and citizens of the importance of this broad perspective.

The drainage issue in California has been unresolved for decades, and the San Joaquin Valley Drainage Program (SJVDP) is only the latest in a series of attempts to study and solve this problem. It is an especially important effort right now, however, because of the realization that similar irrigation-related problems are occurring elsewhere and other problem solvers will look to the SJVDP as a model. The effort being led by the SJVDP is not perfect—in fact, it suffers from numerous inefficiencies and conflicts. But the program has broadened the scientific knowledge base and has served to focus public discussion. There are lessons to be learned from the San Joaquin Valley experience that can help make future efforts to solve irrigation-induced water quality problems more successful.

During the committee's oversight of the SJVDP, it became apparent that this committee defined the problem in the San Joaquin Valley differently than did the staff at the SJVDP and many of the people involved in the dilemma. Throughout its discussions, the committee implicitly defined the problem this way: **irrigation in the San Joaquin Valley without adequate drainage has negative effects on the environment and society.** **The committee's general statement of the goals that alternative responses should strive to achieve is as follows: take steps to avoid or minimize further environmental degradation caused by irrigation water in the valley and recognize that irrigation has negative as well as positive social values.** The committee refrained from emphasizing or expanding its own definition of the problem because, as is stressed many times in this report, this step must be an integral part of a process that must involve all the affected parties. A committee of outsiders cannot accomplish this task.

In the committee's view (see Appendix C), however, the participants in the San Joaquin Valley have not adequately defined the problem. The SJVDP articulated four goals—maintaining crop production, enhancing wildlife habitat, improving water quality, and ensuring public health—but setting goals is not the same as defining problems. Furthermore, problem definition should occur before goal setting. Although the SJVDP has not expressly chosen one of those goals as a top priority, this committee believes it did so indirectly through choices of research emphasis, funding priorities, and in the language in SJVDP documents. Given the program's site-specific perspective and intense local political and social pressures, it is understandable that the program has struggled to bring a broad view to its efforts. As a result, however, the problem has been implicitly defined too narrowly. Many of the participants from California would argue that the problem was agriculturally focused: **environmental damage associated with irrigation drainage is threatening the vitality of agriculture in the San Joaquin Valley.**

This committee sees the sometimes negative environmental impacts associated with irrigation in arid regions as a generic problem that the nation must be better prepared to address. Its recommendations are drawn from a wide range of technical expertise and are aimed at policymakers, project managers, and the public. The committee has not attempted a step-by-step assessment of culpability for the events at Kesterson National Wildlife Refuge (NWR). This was not its mandate and would not help advance the cause of good scientific or policy decisionmaking; nor has the committee provided a detailed critique of the SJVDP's success in finding solutions to the area's problems, because that process is still ongoing. Instead, the committee has focused on two related but independent classes of recommendations.

The first set of recommendations focuses on planning issues and study design. These recommendations suggest methods that should be used when formulating effective responses to irrigation-related water quality problems wherever they may arise. The second set of recommendations addresses policy issues and the opportunities for national action. These are extrapolated from events in the San Joaquin Valley and outline actions that can be implemented by federal and/or state governments to minimize the negative impacts associated with irrigation.

The committee presents these recommendations with the thought that they can help foster awareness of the problems caused by irrigation drainage and can guide decisionmakers in seeking equitable, effective solutions. It is virtually inevitable that additional irrigation-induced water quality problems will appear in the future, as will other environmental problems of a similar nature, and it would indeed be unfortunate if the experience gained from the work in the San Joaquin Valley went unrecognized and unheeded.

PLANNING ISSUES RELATED TO
IRRIGATION-INDUCED WATER QUALITY PROBLEMS

- Federal and state agencies should strive to use sound study design when trying to resolve irrigation-induced water quality problems. Sound study design should emphasize a formal systems approach, be responsive to change, and recognize the dynamic properties of the hydrologic system.

- Federal and state agencies responding to irrigation-related problems should develop an action plan that carefully evaluates the alternative responses available and that reflects increasing scientific understanding of ecosystems. They must work to promote public participation, reconcile competing societal needs, balance economic and non-economic costs, and consider the possibility of institutional and legal changes.

- Federal and state agencies should choose a course of action only after all the identified alternatives have been examined and displayed openly. There must be a clear understanding that "win-win" solutions capable of satisfying all parties are rare and that options often need to be site- or region-specific. All options present economic trade-offs and value choices, so that judgments are necessary.

- Federal and state agencies involved in efforts to find solutions to irrigation-induced water quality problems should pay particular attention to the feasibility of implementation. A sound implementation strategy should assure adequate and stable funding, coordination among agencies and levels of government, effective enforcement, competent personnel with clear responsibilities, and well-defined channels for citizen input and review.

- Federal and state agencies, including the U.S. Department of Agriculture and the U.S. Environmental Protection Agency, need to be actively involved in some type of interagency program to regularly monitor the impacts of irrigation on water quality at all major irrigation projects. This program should contain elements devoted to anticipating future problems and to monitoring water quality over the long term. The National Irrigation

Water Quality Program, or some equivalent, could perform these functions indefinitely. Components of the San Joaquin Valley Drainage Program also will need to be continued.

One clear lesson that can be drawn from the Kesterson experience and applied broadly to irrigation-related water quality problems is the importance of good problem solving and study design. Fundamental to this is the use of a systems approach. Formal systems analysis is necessary to ensure integrity in data collection and interpretation, and it enhances the linkages between study components. Only by thoroughly addressing the biological, physical, economic, institutional, legal, and social issues and the relationships among these factors can the problem be reduced to manageable dimensions. Formal attention is also necessary to understand the different spatial and temporal scales present and to identify the hierarchical levels operating. Such an approach needs to be interdisciplinary (as differentiated from multidisciplinary) and needs to incorporate a breadth of relevant expertise. The acquisition of the information required to respond to complex environmental problems such as these requires meticulous attention to data quality (quality assurance and quality control). A monitoring system should be established and maintained to assess changes in the system throughout the study period and beyond.

The need for sound study design cannot be overstated. Perhaps the most commonly avoided element of the study process is the need to assess and display all the possible alternative responses, even those that may be publicly or politically unpalatable. The point is not to force an unwanted solution, but to ensure credibility for the alternative that ultimately is chosen. Successful problem resolution requires that the interests of all the parties be considered and the costs allocated in an equitable fashion. Only by openly discussing all the potential options, including their costs, benefits, and trade-offs, can the public have faith in the final decision.

Development of a process to manage the inevitable conflicting demands that occur in interdisciplinary studies is a necessity. Policymakers must recognize that rarely are there any "win-win" solutions that will fully satisfy all parties. In the final consensus, all parties gain and lose some benefits.

In the San Joaquin Valley, for instance, the option of ocean disposal of the selenium-contaminated drainage water has been essentially ignored, and the option of land retirement has been treated cautiously at best. Although these options may be impractical for economic, legal, political, or social reasons, they should not be eliminated a priori as alternatives. There are lessons to be learned from an analysis of all possible choices. Even if an option appears to be unacceptable, the physical, biological, and economic consequences should still be assessed and compared with other options. Perhaps some innovative solution would unexpectedly prove possible. More likely, the exercise would spell out clearly the disadvantages and help in the process of selecting a different choice. Unpopular options should receive fair attention and objective study, and the local, regional, and national consequences should be openly assessed.

The fragmentation of interests of the different institutional players has been a major management problem in the San Joaquin Valley situation. These different institutions reflect the concerns and interests of various client groups. These specialized interest groups have limited perspectives, and each special interest by itself was not likely to develop an effective long-term management plan to address the complex problems faced. A lasting solution can emerge only by bringing all competing interests together to air their concerns openly and develop solutions.

A public participation program should draw all affected interest groups into an exchange of views with the involved agencies and should move toward resolving the conflict through consensus building. Public participation builds confidence that the decision process was fair and complete. In the SJVDP, a citizens' advisory committee was not established until mid-1987, more than 2 years into the program. The committee might have been more effective (in terms of problem definition and study plan development) if it had been created sooner. The absence of this feature was somewhat frustrating to the public and may have given the impression that the problem-solving process was more "political" than it actually was.

Environmental concerns are changing, and protective measures have become more acceptable because of our increasing understanding of ecosystems, changing societal values, and recurrent revelations of significant environmental problems. Strategies to solve irrigation-induced water quality problems should acknowledge society's diverse interest groups and conflicting environmental viewpoints. They also should respond to the increasing pressures on the environment and include flexibility for responding to future change.

Uniform solutions are seldom applicable over wide areas. Geologic and hydrologic properties can vary dramatically, even over short distances. Resource managers should recognize the unique characteristics of specific sites and devise management practices adapted to these local characteristics. This will help provide more effective and palatable packages of solutions. However, such local management practices also need to recognize regional and national needs.

Successful problem resolution requires that the interests of all the parties be considered and the costs allocated in an equitable fashion. In assessing the equity issue, it is important that all costs and impacts be explicitly recognized. The interest groups affected by irrigated agriculture have diverse environmental values, different sociopolitical perspectives, and differing levels of capital investments that are threatened by irrigation-induced water quality problems.

Legal and institutional changes will prove necessary to solve the water management problems of the future, although the specific nature of these changes will require careful study and planning. Irrigation systems have evolved with supporting institutions that provide a protective legal framework for water rights and land tenure. The inertia of these entities sometimes severely constrains the approaches considered possible for dealing with irrigation-induced water quality problems.

POLICY ISSUES RELATED TO
IRRIGATION-INDUCED WATER QUALITY PROBLEMS

- If any major irrigation projects are planned in the future, at the onset federal and state agencies should calculate the costs of drainage for irrigation return flows and should commit funds to build and maintain the system.

- Federal and state agencies should design and implement management systems that minimize the adverse impacts of irrigation, especially those that occur when irrigating land in closed basins, and acknowledge the inevitable ecological trade-offs that accompany irrigation.

- Federal and state agencies should systematically monitor all major irrigation projects for substances that could cause water quality problems, including pesticides and fertilizers as well as trace elements.

- Federal and state agencies that facilitate or regulate irrigation should periodically calculate and publicize the environmental costs as well as the agricultural benefits associated with irrigation, and should work to accommodate the nation's increasing commitment to protecting environmental values.

- Irrigation return flows should not be exempt from federal and state water quality regulations, and such regulations should be enforced.

- Federal and state agencies should increase their efforts to provide water supplies for wildlife, enhance and enlarge wildlife habitats, and protect the biological and recreational values associated with in-stream flows and good water quality.

- Federal and state agencies should acknowledge all external costs—including social and environmental costs—when calculating the costs and benefits of agricultural subsidies.

- Federal and state agencies should identify irrigated lands that are degrading water quality significantly and should implement cost-effective, environmentally sound actions to correct or minimize the degradation. Such a program would incorporate a range of alternative approaches for preventing, mitigating, and treating irrigation drainage problems. This would include, if necessary, phasing out production on particularly problematic lands.

Irrigated agriculture remains the largest water user in the West. But numerous other, competing interests are increasing pressure on a diminishing and deteriorating water resource. With this competition comes an increasing need, real and perceived, to find solutions acceptable not only to the irrigation interests but to other parties as well.

An obvious, but curiously ignored, lesson reinforced by the events at Kesterson NWR is that federal and state agencies should not plan or build an irrigation project unless they are prepared to finish it. Drainage systems are best designed and installed after the water table in the area has risen, when the modified local hydrology can be better understood. Even so, the cost of the drainage system should be estimated at project initiation, and a commitment for completion should be assured. The cost of maintenance also should be included in the original economic analyses and financial commitments.

It is a long- and well-known fact that irrigation in arid lands tends to degrade the quality of the return-flow water by increasing its salinity or nutrient concentrations, or by increasing the concentrations of some substances to toxic levels. These problems are particularly severe in closed basins, where the lack of an outlet inevitably causes environmental degradation as dissolved substances accumulate in the soil, standing water, and ground water. The environmental damage at Kesterson NWR in the San Joaquin Valley, for example, happened as quickly as it did because the irrigation return flows were confined to a closed basin. Management that fails to address ultimate disposal is simply moving the problem from one place to another, or from one generation to the next.

When planning projects where drainage flows will be confined in closed basins, federal and state agencies should be especially careful to design these systems to minimize the adverse effects of ever-increasing salt concentrations. They should recognize that the practice of irrigation will require the ultimate sacrifice of some water quality and ecological values. At present there are no known, practical, technological processes available to repair the damage caused by the buildup of toxic substances in closed basins.

Historically, salinity standards have been seen more as a state and federal responsibility than as the responsibility of individual irrigators. Federal and state agencies should be prepared to provide an adequate level of monitoring at all major irrigation projects as a way of anticipating future problems. Selenium was the natural contaminant that brought the problems in the San Joaquin Valley to public attention, but given the geology of the West, it is only one element among many (e.g., arsenic, boron, cadmium, lead, mercury, and molybdenum) that may already be causing harm at wildlife refuges and in other environments. Attention to pesticide and fertilizer residues will also prove necessary. The government and irrigators should also be aware that current knowledge is incomplete and that the problem-causing elements known today may be joined by others in the future.

Policymakers and program managers should design monitoring systems capable of early identification of incipient environmental, social, and economic problems. They should provide support for the timely interpretation and evaluation of monitoring data. Federal and state agencies with mandates for managing water quality should support sustained research to assess whether management goals are being achieved, and they should provide adequate funding to ensure that corrections can be implemented when problems are identified.

If additional problem areas are identified in the future, the nation will need to be prepared to act. The nature of the response will of course vary depending on the site and on numerous technical, economic, and social variables. However, all attempts to correct or minimize the degradation must be both economically and environmentally sound. Plans to phase out irrigated agriculture on the most problematic lands should be considered if it is not possible or practical to treat or dispose of drainage waters. Planners should keep both short-term and long-term goals in perspective.

Existing water appropriation policy places too little value on the public and beneficial use of in-stream flow. Irrigation in the United States typically is not subject to regulatory control that would protect water quality for other uses. Federal agencies responsible for facilitating irrigation typically do not—but should—consider water quality degradation as a cost of water use. Federal and state agencies responsible for protecting and enhancing wildlife must redouble their efforts to protect and increase the supply of quality habitats. Those agencies that regulate water use should dedicate sufficient water to in-stream use to protect biological and recreation resources.

The U.S. Department of the Interior has facilitated numerous irrigation projects in the western United States that may produce environmental degradation similar to that observed at Kesterson NWR. The nation must be better prepared to deal with irrigation-induced water quality problems that will occur on both public and private lands. The U.S. Bureau of Reclamation (USBR) provided water for about 12 million acres in 1986, which is only about 25 percent of the West's irrigation water. But problems are occurring or are likely to occur also on the remaining 75 percent of land irrigated through private or state funds. If the focus is solely on the USBR, potential and serious problems may be ignored elsewhere.

RESPONDING TO IRRIGATION-INDUCED WATER QUALITY PROBLEMS: A SHARED RESPONSIBILITY

The events that occurred in California's San Joaquin Valley were caused by a combination of human and natural factors, and they proved to be an especially poignant reminder of the interrelationships between people and the land and water resources upon which they depend. They are also a harbinger of what the future holds for irrigated agriculture in other areas of the West and the world.

In its attempts to provide guidance to the SJVDP, this committee has pointed out many flaws and problems with that group's effort to find a solution to the irrigation-induced water quality degradation in the San Joaquin Valley. The criticisms, conveyed in letter reports (see Appendix C), were directed to help the SJVDP carry out its tasks. They also were intended to help establish a model to guide the effective conduct of similar study efforts in the future. The issues cited included problems with inadequate expertise, inappropriate study design, and quality assurance and quality control. Inadequate attention to critical legal, institutional, and economic issues early in the study was also a weakness.

The committee would like to point out, however, that despite these varied criticisms, there is a need for an interagency approach like that embodied in the SJVDP. The SJVDP has been a serious attempt to seek solutions to a difficult problem, one that incorporated two particularly essential elements: interagency coordination and public participation. The SJVDP has generated new geological and biological data that broaden the scientific understanding of drainage issues. In addition, it has provided a forum to increase public understanding of the scope and severity of the problems associated with irrigation drainage. The SJVDP also has helped explain the importance of drainage for the future of irrigation in the San Joaquin Valley. Considering the difficulty of the situation and its history, the committee appreciated the efforts of California and the Department of the Interior to work together toward problem resolution.

The efforts under way by the Department of the Interior's National Irrigation Water Quality Program are also important as part of the nation's overall response to these types of problems. This effort is a step already under way to meet one of the principal arguments that serves as a foundation for this report: other irrigation-induced water quality problems will be discovered in the future, and the nation must do a better job of identifying, understanding, and responding to these problems.

One fact made clear during this committee's oversight of the San Joaquin Valley Drainage Program is that finding a solution to the valley's drainage problems, and to similar problems elsewhere in the West, is not merely a technical question. Indeed, the more difficult questions are often political, social, and economic. In all cases, however, the various components are intimately interrelated. Only by defining and addressing the system as a whole, and realistically assessing its complexity, can progress toward real and lasting solutions be made.

The U.S. Bureau of Reclamation, which received considerable attention in this report because of its primary role in the Kesterson NWR experience, is not alone in facing the significant challenges arising from irrigation-induced water quality problems. The problems are not all caused by federal and state agencies, nor can they necessarily be solved at those levels alone. The federal and state agencies involved in irrigation are mandated to carry out the will of the public, and so the ultimate responsibility for solving these types of problems is one that the public shares.

APPENDIXES

Appendix A
Biographical Sketches of
Committee Members

JAN van SCHILFGAARDE received his Ph.D. in soil physics and agricultural engineering in 1954. At present he is associate director of the Northern Plains Area, Agricultural Research Service in Fort Collins, Colorado. Previously he was director of the U.S. Salinity Laboratory, Department of Agriculture, Riverside, California. He has published over 60 documents, primarily in soil and water management, and is a member of American Society of Agricultural Engineering, American Society of Civil Engineering, American Society of Agronomists, and the Soil Conservation Society of America. Jan van Schilfgaarde is also a member of the National Research Council's Board on Agriculture and a member of the National Academy of Engineering.

WILLIAM H. ALLAWAY received his Ph.D. in 1945 from Iowa State University and an honorary D.Sc. from the University of Nebraska in 1971. He has been a professor (soils) at Iowa State; director, U.S. Plant, Soil and Nutrition Laboratory, U.S. Department of Agriculture; and advisor to the U.S. Chilean minister of agriculture. His research has centered on soil chemistry and on trace elements (especially selenium) in soils, plants, and animals. He is professor emeritus, Cornell University.

ERNEST E. ANGINO received his Ph.D. in geochemistry in 1961 from the University of Kansas, where he is professor of geology and chairman of that department. He has been a member of the National Research Council's U.S. National Committee on Geochemistry and vice-chairman, technical advisory committee, Committee on Resources and Development, Federal Power Commission. He was awarded the Antarctic Service Medal by the U.S. Department of Defense. His research has involved trace element complexing in natural waters and sediment-water interactions.

MARGRIET F. CASWELL received a Ph.D. in agricultural and resource economics in 1983 at the University of California, Berkeley. She is assistant professor of economics and environmental studies, University of California, Santa Barbara. The majority of her recent research concerns agricultural water issues in California, with particular interest in the interactions between water demand, waste water production, and irrigation technology choice. She has been a postgraduate research economist for the Giannini Foundation of Agricultural Economics, a lecturer in the economics of resource conservation, and a consultant.

EDWIN H. CLARK II received a B.S. in engineering from Yale University in 1960, an M.S. (water resources engineering) and M.A. (economics) in 1966 from Princeton University, and a Ph.D. in economics from Princeton in 1971. Dr. Clark is an expert in water quality and agricultural management issues. He has worked as a consulting engineer for Harza and did research in Pakistan relative to water supplies for agriculture. He taught economics at Williams College and served as a senior staff member at the Council on Environmental Quality through 1978. For three years (until 1981), Dr. Clark served as deputy director of the U.S. Environmental Protection Agency's Office of Pesticides and Toxic Substances, where he was concurrently a special assistant to the administrator. Until recently, he was vice president of The Conservation Foundation's water resources program. He is now secretary of the Department of Natural Resources and Environmental Control for the state of Delaware.

CHARLES T. DuMARS received his B.S. from Oregon State University and his J.D. from Arizona State University in 1969. He is a member of the bar in both New Mexico and Arizona. At present, he is professor of law at the University of New Mexico. Previously he was chief counsel of the New Mexico Legal Rights Demonstration Land Grant Project. His area of expertise is in water law.

WILFORD R. GARDNER received a Ph.D. in physics from Iowa State College in 1953. His research has been in measurement of soil moisture by neutron scattering; soil physics; movement of fluids in porous media; soil-water plant relations; soil salinity; plant biophysics; and environmental physics. He is dean, College of Natural Resources, University of California at Berkeley. Previously he was with the department of soils, water, and engineering at the University of Arizona, Tucson. He has been a National Science Foundation senior fellow at Cambridge University and a Fulbright lecturer, University of Ghent. Dr. Gardner is a member of the National Academy of Sciences.

ROLF HARTUNG received his Ph.D. in 1964 at the University of Michigan, and in 1980 he was designated diplomat, American Board of Toxicology. At the University of Michigan he is a professor of environmental toxicology in the Department of Environmental and Industrial Health. Previously he was chairman of the toxicology program there.

CHARLES D. D. HOWARD received M.S. degrees from the University of Alberta (1962) and the Massachusetts Institute of Technology (1966). He is president of the consulting engineering firm Charles Howard and Associates, Ltd., located in Victoria, British Columbia, and has specialized in water resources systems analysis. He has developed innovative mathematical and computer methods for water resources operations and planning, including implementation of water quality models for nonpoint runoff and in-stream processes related to irrigation return flows and transport of hazardous chemicals. He has served agencies of the United Nations and Canadian federal, provincial, and municipal governments and has participated in many studies for U.S. agencies and utilities.

L. DOUGLAS JAMES received B.S.C.E., M.S.C.E., and Ph.D. (1965) degrees from Stanford University. He has held several teaching and consulting positions and is director of the Utah Water Research Laboratory at Utah State University. He has broad expertise in water resources planning and flood hydraulics and was chairman of the National Research Council's Committee on a Levee Policy for the National Flood Insurance Program, whose report was provided to the Federal Emergency Management Agency in October 1982. He is also a former member of the National Research Council's Water Science and Technology Board.

WILLIAM M. LEWIS, JR., received his Ph.D. in zoology with a minor in mathematics from Indiana University in 1973. He was a research associate and subsequently adjunct assistant professor of zoology at the University of Georgia between 1973 and 1974. In 1974, he moved to the University of Colorado at Boulder as assistant professor of biology. At the University of Colorado he held the rank of assistant professor from 1978 to 1982 and of professor after 1982. He is director of the University of Colorado Center for Limnology. Dr. Lewis was a Guggenheim fellow in 1980 to 1981 and has previously served on National Research Council committees, including the Water Science and Technology Board's Committee on Glen

Canyon Environmental Studies. His interests include aquatic food chains, the trophic status of lakes, the chemistry of surface water, mass transport by large rivers, and interactions between floodplains and rivers.

ROBERT R. MEGLEN received his Ph.D. in physical chemistry from the University of Colorado in 1971. He is director of the Analytical Laboratory of the Center for Environmental Sciences and is also adjunct professor in the chemistry department at the University of Colorado at Denver. His research interests are in the area of analytical applications of optical spectroscopy and ion chromatography. For many years he has conducted trace element research on a variety of environmental problems, including energy development, nutrition, drinking water standards, and ground and surface water contamination. Dr. Meglen was appointed to membership on the Water Science and Technology Board in 1988.

FRANCOIS M. M. MOREL received his Ph.D. in engineering sciences from California Institute of Technology in 1971. He is currently graduate officer, department of civil engineering, Massachusetts Institute of Technology, Cambridge. His fields of interest lie in theoretical and experimental studies on the effects and fate of chemical pollutants; computer modeling of chemical characteristics of natural and polluted waters; coordination chemistry and photochemistry of trace metals in natural waters; interactions between the chemistry and microbiota in aquatic systems; and trace metal nutrition and toxicity in phytoplankton. He has served on a National Research Council panel on marine mineral technology and was a member of the committee on ocean waste transportation.

ISHWAR P. MURARKA is manager of Electric Power Research Institute's Land and Water Quality Studies Program. Previously, he was an environmental scientist at the Argonne National Laboratory and a faculty member at Northern Illinois University and North Carolina State University. He holds several advanced degrees, including a Ph.D. in soil science (Oregon State University, 1971). He has expertise in waste management, pollutants in the environment, and subsurface water quality. He is active in professional organizations and has published 70 scientific papers, many related to ground water quality. He is a consultant to the Science Advisory Board of the U.S. Environmental Protection Agency and is a Certified Professional Soil Scientist.

OSCAR E. OLSON received a Ph.D. in biochemistry from the University of Wisconsin in 1948. He is professor emeritus at South Dakota State University. He has been dean of the graduate school, South Dakota State University; visiting professor, Institute of Enzyme Research, University of

Wisconsin/Madison; visiting scientist, U.S. Plant, Soil, and Nutrition Laboratory, New York; member of the National Research Council subcommittee on nutrient and toxic elements in water; member of the NRC panel on agricultural uses of water; and member of the NRC panel on medical and biological effects of environmental pollutants—selenium. His research has dealt with selenium and nitrate poisoning and calcium metabolism in poultry.

W. SCOTT OVERTON received an M.S. in wildlife management in 1950 from Virginia Polytechnic Institute and a Ph.D. in experimental statistics from North Carolina State University in 1964. He has been professor of forest science at Oregon State University and visiting professor at Emory University and Cornell University. His research interests are in statistics and ecology, spatial distributions, population dynamics, evolutionary and growth processes, modeling, general systems theory, ecosystem theory, and resource management. He is with the Department of Fisheries and Wildlife, Oregon State University.

ALBERT L. PAGE received his B.A. from the University of California at Riverside in 1956 and his Ph.D. in soil science from the University of California at Davis in 1960. His area of expertise is in soil chemistry. Presently he is professor of soil science at the University of California, Riverside. Previously he was director of the University of California Division of Agricultural Sciences, Kerney Foundation of Soil Science. His research interests include chemical and mineralogical properties of soils; chemistry of hydrolyzable metals in colloid systems; ion exchange equilibrium; and environmental trace metal contamination. He was a Guggenheim and Fullbright fellow and is a member of the Soil Science Society of America and the American Society of Agronomy.

MERILYN B. REEVES is a member of the Board of Directors of the League of Women Voters of the United States. She chairs the Advocacy Issues Committee for the national league. From 1980 to 1984 she served as the natural resources coordinator of the national board. She has been a member of the National Drinking Water Advisory Council; chair of the State of Maryland Hazardous Substances and Low-Level Nuclear Waste Council; member of the Department of Energy's Environmental Committee; and member of the Maryland and Chesapeake Bay Legislative Advisory Commission. She holds an M.S. degree from Northern State College in South Dakota.

KENNETH D. SCHMIDT received a Ph.D. in hydrology from the University of Arizona, Tucson, in 1971. He is a registered geologist in the states of California, Arizona, and Oregon and a ground water quality consultant in Phoenix. Since 1964 he has worked on numerous ground water investigations in the San Joaquin Valley. He has participated in the Basin 5D studies by the California Regional Water Quality Control Board, evaluating salt loading to ground water, impacts of irrigation on salinity, and fertilizer contributions to nitrate concentration. He has evaluated the impacts of irrigation on ground water quality as a member of an irrigation and drainage division task force of the American Society of Civil Engineers. He has also performed a detailed evaluation of the effect of irrigation on ground water quality in the Salt River valley of Arizona.

R. RHODES TRUSSELL received his Ph.D. in 1972 at the University of California, Berkeley. His principal expertise lies in the areas of water quality and water treatment for domestic and industrial use as well as chemistry. He has served on a National Research Council committee on drinking water additives and as technical chairman, American Water Works Association's Particulates Committee.

DANIEL E. WILLARD is an ecologist and wetlands biologist. He received an A.B. in biology (1959) from Stanford University and a Ph.D. in zoology (1966) from the University of California at Davis. He taught zoology at the University of Texas from 1966 to 1970 and then at the University of Wisconsin through 1977. He has taught at the University of Oregon's Institute of Marine Biology and at Cornell University's Shoals Marine Laboratory. Currently he is professor and director of environmental science and policy programs in the School of Public and Environmental Affairs and professor of biology at Indiana University, Bloomington.

Appendix B
Calendar of the Committee's Activities
(May 1985 to August 1989)

May 29-31, 1985

Full committee, Sacramento, California.
First meeting. Introductions, reviewed National Research Council (NRC) policy, and discussed overall goals and expectations. Included technical briefings to orient committee members to the issues.

July 31-August 2, 1985

Full committee, Sacramento, California.
Second meeting. Met with the San Joaquin Valley Drainage Program's (SJVDP) Policy and Management Committee; reviewed the U.S. Bureau of Reclamation's (USBR) Plan of Study and Plan of Work; listened to technical briefings from the U.S. Geological Survey (USGS), the U.S. Fish and Wildlife Service (USFWS), and USBR. Presented specific suggestions regarding SJVDP management.

September 20, 1985

Working group of full committee, Sacramento, California.
Selected members met to draft a letter report as follow-up to the committee's July/August meeting.

December 12-13, 1985

Full committee, Sacramento, California.

Third meeting. Statements of task for four sub-committees were discussed and approved (public health, quality assurance and quality control, systems analysis, and treatment technologies). Received briefings on economic and institutional issues, activities of the University of California Salinity/Drainage Task Force, and public participation.

March 27-28, 1986   Full committee, Washington, D.C.
Fourth meeting. Received update on subcommittee activities, SJVDP activities, events at Kesterson National Wildlife Refuge (NWR), and progress toward citizens' advisory committee. Committee reflected on its purpose and best way to carry out its responsibilities, clearly stating that it saw its role as broader than the SJVDP evaluation alone.

April 4, 1986   Subcommittee on Public Health, Sacramento, California.
First meeting. Introductions and review of NRC policies. Three areas addressed were hazards associated with selenium and other organics and inorganics, exposure, and risk communication (mechanisms to identify health issues and provide public health services). Related briefings by county and state health officials.

July 17-18, 1986   Full committee, Boulder, Colorado.
Fifth meeting. Committee discussed its role in advising the U.S. Department of the Interior's program on irrigation-related water quality problems throughout the West; decided to write an interim report; and agreed to establish a subcommittee on economics and policy. Met with the new program manager of the SJVDP.

October 22, 1986   Subcommittee on Quality Assurance and Quality Control, Sacramento, California.
First meeting. Introductions, review of purpose and NRC policies, parent committee activities, and tasks for meeting. Received SJVDP briefings on proposed quality assurance plan and critiqued

plan. Urged SJVDP to appoint a quality assurance and quality control officer.

October 23-24, 1986
Full committee, Sacramento, California.
Sixth meeting. The committee heard updates from subcommittee chairs, the Policy and Management Committee, the SJVDP, scientists studying cleanup options at Kesterson NWR, and representatives of the U.S. Department of the Interior's new National Irrigation Water Quality Program (NIWQP) and Westlands Water District. They were briefed on the status of research being conducted by the USFWS. Planning for an interim report continued.

October 28-29, 1986
Subcommittee on Treatment Technologies, Berkeley, California.
First meeting. Introductions, review of purpose and NRC policies, and update on full committee activities. Subcommittee heard extensive briefings regarding the technological alternatives available to control water quality degradation (including on-farm management, treatment technologies, and disposal alternatives) from state and federal agencies, university and private researchers, and the SJVDP.

January 29-30, 1987
Subcommittee on Economics and Policy, Santa Barbara, California.
First meeting. Introductions, discussion of purpose and NRC policies, and orientation to full committee's activities. Heard briefings on public participation, upcoming SJVDP documents, trends in agricultural policy, and financial perspectives. Stressed need for SJVDP to use a good planning process and planned a letter report. SJVDP requested future review of "Phase I" document.

February 26-27, 1987
Subcommittee on Systems Analysis, Corvallis, Oregon.
First meeting. Introductions, review of purpose and NRC policies, and parent committee activities. Systems analysis and integrated planning are expected to be essential to the SJVDP

problem-solving endeavor. Reviewed SJVDP document, *Plan Formulation Process*. Briefed regarding SJVDP-sponsored workshops on management practices, and regarding the program's modeling efforts.

March 4-6, 1987   Full committee, Tucson, Arizona.
Seventh meeting. The committee was briefed by the SJVDP program manager, heard subcommittee updates, and continued to plan its interim report. Approximately 50 USGS, USFWS, and USBR scientists took part in presentations on ongoing research efforts related to irrigation drainage problems.

June 2-3, 1987   Full committee, Denver, Colorado.
Eighth meeting. The committee stressed the need for Quality Assurance and Quality Control for the SJVDP, listened to a presentation by two San Joaquin Valley landowners, and discussed the evolving outline and draft of its interim report. Small working groups met to further develop these ideas.

June 9-10, 1987   Subcommittee on Economics and Policy, Washington, D.C.
Second meeting. Discussed importance of economics and policy perspective in both the SJVDP and the NIWQP. Heard presentations on water marketing and Congress; received briefing on SJVDP activities and proposed research; met jointly with Subcommittee on Systems Analysis to coordinate objectives. Briefed on parent committee activities.

June 10-11, 1987   Subcommittee on Systems Analysis, Washington, D.C.
Second Meeting. Update on parent committee activities, including progress of written report and request for eventual subcommittee review. The subcommittee's continuing goal is to ensure that systems thinking is woven into SJVDP efforts. One day was spent in joint session with the Subcommittee on Economics and Policy, listening to and responding to SJVDP briefings on models

and the status of the planning studies.

August 10-11, 1987   Subcommittee on Economics and Policy, Sacramento, California.
Third meeting. Broad discussions of the SJVDP's efforts to address legal, economic, and institutional elements of the drainage problem. Reviewed SJVDP's "Phase I" document. Stressed importance of a broad, national perspective. Recommended addition of staff with legal expertise.

October 1-2, 1987   Full committee, San Francisco, California.
Ninth meeting. The two primary goals for this meeting were to discuss committee members' review of seven NIWQP field screening studies and to continue drafting the interim report. The subcommittee chairs all reported, and there was some discussion of the impending completion of CII-WQP's contract (due to expire March 31, 1988), contract renewal, and potential changes in the composition of the committee.

December 3-4, 1987   Subcommittee on Economics and Policy, San Francisco, California.
Fourth meeting. Heard briefings on parent committee activities and extension of original cooperative agreement, plus updates on SJVDP and NIWQP activities. Reviewed SJVDP's *Developing Options* report. Heard presentations from contractors conducting economics and policy-related research for the SJVDP.

January 28-29, 1988   Full committee, Tucson, Arizona.
Tenth meeting. The committee discussed the planned 2-year extension of its contract, its goals for this extension, and changes in membership. They reviewed their draft report, deciding to combine the two volumes into one, and worked to develop recommendations. The SJVDP program manager discussed the possibility of a jointly sponsored symposium in spring 1989.

May 5-6, 1988   Full committee, Washington, D.C.
Eleventh meeting. Beginning of 2-year extension of committee activities. Four members rotated off committee; five new members were introduced. Discussed future goals; continued work on report.

June 23-24, 1988   Joint meeting of Subcommittee on Economics and
                            Policy and Subcommittee on Systems Analysis,
                            Berkeley, California.
                            Fifth meeting for Economics and Policy; third
                            meeting for Systems Analysis. Subcommittees re-
                            viewed SJVDP draft, *Procedures for Formulating
                            and Evaluating Drainage Management Plans for
                            the San Joaquin Valley.* Also heard an update on
                            SJVDP institutional studies.

September 29-30, 1988   Full committee, Irvine, California.
                            Twelfth meeting. The committee was briefed on
                            technical aspects of the cleanup at Kesterson
                            NWR, discussed water policy issues with the chair-
                            man of California State Water Resources Control
                            Board, and continued to revise its report.

March 8-10, 1989   Full Committee, Albuquerque, New Mexico.
                            Thirteenth meeting. The committee held a joint
                            meeting with NIWQP staff and heard mid-course
                            briefings on 15 studies of potential problem sites
                            in the West. Also were briefed by SJVDP pro-
                            gram manager regarding efforts to develop alter-
                            nate solutions.

April 6-7, 1989   Subcommittee on Economics, Policy, and Systems
                            Analysis (formerly two separate subcommittees),
                            San Francisco, California.
                            Sixth meeting. The subcommittee was briefed on
                            recent SJVDP activities related to social, institu-
                            tional, and legal issues, with special attention to
                            future legal analyses. It also continued to follow
                            the SJVDP's development of the WADE com-
                            puter model.

July 6-7, 1989   Full committee, Irvine, California.
                            Fourteenth meeting. The committee discussed
                            the methods and needs of the NIWQP's long-
                            term monitoring activities and began planning a
                            culminating workshop to encourage western state
                            policymakers to address irrigation-related water
                            quality problems. It continued to monitor the
                            SJVDP's activities.

Appendix C
Summary of the Committee's Letter
Reports (May 1985 to August 1989)

The Committee on Irrigation-Induced Water Quality Problems (CIIWQP) and its subcommittees chose to use letter reports as their primary mechanism to formally convey recommendations and comments to the San Joaquin Valley Drainage Program (SJVDP) and the National Irrigation Water Quality Program (NIWQP). These letter reports were issued in response to briefings, draft documents, and other requests for assistance. They often provided specific scientific advice, but they also were used to convey the committee's overall sense of the adequacy and breadth of the ongoing research program. Although it is not possible to track precisely the responses to the reports, overall it was felt that the letter reports have had significant impacts.

October 1985   CIIWQP

Following briefings about the SJVDP, this letter report calls for improved coordination of research activities, better overall program management, and a program for public participation. Other areas of concern include the need for data management and the ongoing interpretation of data; the importance of quality assurance and quality control; the need to consider agricultural chemicals in the design of analytical studies; the significance of economic, legal, and institutional constraints on the choice of solutions; and the need to consider on-farm management options.

143

April 1986   CIIWQP

Responding to briefings provided by the University of California research program related to irrigation drainage problems in the San Joaquin Valley, this letter report praises the research addressing on-farm water and salinity management, transport processes, and trace element chemistry. However, the committee believes the university researchers should be better integrated into the overall SJVDP research program. Research areas requiring attention include public health concerns, economic evaluations of potential alternative solutions, and the long-term impacts on ecosystems. The committee urges that recommendations from its October 1985 letter report be implemented as soon as possible (such as development of a strong public participation program; full consideration of economic, institutional, and legal factors; investigation of public health concerns; and development of a quality assurance and quality control program and a data-management program).

June 1986   Subcommittee on Public Health

This letter report reviews the research proposed by the SJVDP related to public health. Generally, the report is favorable, but it identifies some deficiencies in five areas: (1) the need for a more coherent conceptual approach; (2) identification of hazards; (3) exposure assessment; (4) integration of public health delivery services; and (5) the establishment of a public health subcommittee within the SJVDP.

June 1986   Subcommittee on Quality Assurance
                  and Quality Control

This letter report reviews a draft quality assurance plan for the SJVDP. It is critical of the plan and provides many suggestions for improvement in the areas of (1) quality assurance policy and management; (2) data quality objectives and sampling procedures; (3) analytical procedures; (4) data reduction, validation, and reporting; and (5) performance and system audits. The subcommittee stresses that a well-designed quality assurance plan is essential.

September 1986   CIIWQP

This letter report asks the SJVDP to assess a proposal for the cleanup of Kesterson Reservoir made by the Lawrence Berkeley Laboratory of the University of California regarding maintaining flooded conditions. The committee recommends that basic studies of the biological cycling of selenium in saline and alkaline aquatic ecosystems be given high priority. It recommends that a thorough monitoring system be established to assess the impacts of this management approach on plants, animals, sediments, and water.

February 1987   Subcommittee on Public Health

This is a supplement to the June 1986 letter report from this subcommittee that recommends that as the SJVDP evaluates the feasibility and desirability of various solutions, it should explicitly address the public health concerns that might be raised by such actions.

March 1987   Subcommittee on Quality Assurance
                       and Quality Control

This letter report strongly recommends that the SJVDP hire an experienced quality assurance and quality control manager as soon as possible. It also stresses that data management must be performed so that it ensures that useful information is not lost. The committee raises concerns that the quality control protocol for plant tissue appears to lack the rigor of other protocols (such as those for water, soil, sediment, and animal tissue).

July 1987   CIIWQP

This letter report commends the SJVDP for making progress, especially for establishing a citizens' advisory committee. It urges the addition of a quality assurance and quality control officer and an experienced research biologist. The committee still believes that the SJVDP gives inadequate attention to comprehensive, integrated planning, and it stresses that the SJVDP must consider all the available options, even those that are politically unpalatable.

July 1987   Subcommittee on Economics and Policy

This letter report reminds the SJVDP that the interactions between human activities and the environment cannot be ignored and that technology must be seen in light of evolving social and economic systems. It advises the SJVDP to develop an analytical methodology to identify diverse and often conflicting environmental and economic considerations; examine equity issues; and broadly evaluate the general public policy issues involved in the alternative solutions being studied. The committee also stresses the importance of addressing legal issues.

May 1988   Subcommittee on Economics and Policy

This letter report comments on the SJVDP publication *Developing Options: An Overview of Efforts to Solve Agricultural Drainage and Drainage-Related Problems in the San Joaquin Valley.* The report also stresses several points regarding the continued need for a broad focus in the SJVDP's research, the importance of not narrowing the choice of alternative solutions prematurely, and the urgent need to initiate the planned legal and institutional policy analysis.

July 1988   CIIWQP

This letter report to the U.S. Department of the Interior's National Irrigation Water Quality Program (NIWQP)—which was established in 1987—commends the program for its initial efforts to investigate potential irrigation-related water quality problems throughout the West. It reviews the committee's involvement in that ongoing effort, including its review of draft work plans for reconnaissance-level and detailed studies and suggestions to improve them. The letter anticipates the committee's increasing involvement in the NIWQP's activities.

December 1988   Subcommittee on Quality Assurance
                       and Quality Control

This letter report, the third from the Subcommittee on Quality Assurance and Quality Control, stresses the continued importance of quality assurance and quality control activities as the SJVDP winds down its data collection and begins to synthesize information. It also urges the SJVDP to create a central repository of information under a single manager.

May 1989   CIIWQP

This letter report addresses the U.S. Department of the Interior's NIWQP and contains comments in response to a briefing of preliminary data from the NIWQP's second set of reconnaissance studies. It provides suggestions to improve data uniformity and identification of the causes of identified problems, and it calls for the NIWQP to synthesize the myriad data into a comprehensive analysis with systematic conclusions.

August 1989   Subcommittee on Economics, Policy, and Systems Analysis (previously two separate subcommittees)

This letter report to the SJVDP discusses the continued development of the WADE computer model and the need to be frank about both its strengths and weaknesses. The necessity of outside peer review is stressed. The letter also comments on the SJVDP's progress in conducting legal and sociological analyses.

August 1989   CIIWQP

This letter report expresses strong dissatisfaction with the political influences that have directed the SJVDP to look for solutions only within the confines of the San Joaquin Valley. This committee sees this as a short-sighted approach and again urges policymakers to address the long-term impacts of irrigated agriculture.

Index

149